ROCK LONDON
2006

2005

Happy Christmas!
Love
Sarah, Mark
& Calum
xxx
xx
x

ROCK LONDON
2006

The Definitive Guide

Trevor Baker

Aureus

First Published 2005

©2005 Trevor Baker

Trevor Baker has asserted the Author's right under the Copyright, Designs and Patents Act 1988 to be identified as Author of this Work.

All rights reserved. No part of this publication may be reproduced, stored in a retrieval system, or transmitted, in any form or by any means, electronic, mechanical, photocopying or otherwise, without the prior permission of Aureus Publishing.

This publication is printed on paper derived from sustainable forests. The cover is made from recycled material.

The views expressed in this publication are not those of the Publisher.

ISBN-10 : 1 899750 34 7
ISBN-13 : 978-1-899750-34-4

Printed in Great Britain by Athenaeum Press Ltd., Gateshead, Tyne & Wear.

A catalogue record for this book is available from the British Library.

Aureus Publishing Limited
Castle Court
Castle-upon-Alun
St. Bride's Major
Vale of Glamorgan
CF32 0TN

Tel: (01656) 880033 Fax: (01656) 880033
Int. tel: +44 1656 880033 Int. fax: +44 1656 880033

E-mail: sales@aureus.co.uk
Web site: www.aureus.co.uk

INTRODUCTION

A few years ago the biggest problem with writing a guide to London's rock venues would have been the closure of many of them before the book hit the shelves. Now a bigger problem is that new venues are springing up faster than I can get them down on paper.

Landlords from Brixton to Shoreditch have discovered that they can flog more booze by allowing enterprising promoters to put on bands. Clubs have realised that there's a massive demand for live music and, in some areas of the capital, it seems like derelict warehouses can't stay derelict for more than about five minutes without a stage being erected in one corner.

This means that there are more places for bands to play than at any time in the last ten years or more, and more places for fans to go and see them. That's why I decided that there was a need for a kind of Domesday Book of London's rock scene – objectively taking stock of the capital's music venues and coolly separating the wheat from the chaff.

But, after spending about five minutes trying to write that book, I decided that this one will have to do. The opinions in it are just opinions, shamelessly subjective and subject to all of my own particular prejudices, foibles and occasional bouts of drunkenness. I took great pains to try and make sure the 'facts' were properly 'factual' but I apologise for any mistakes that may remain.

All this being said (and I really hope you bought the book before reading this preamble about its flaws) I hope it does serve a small purpose. For new bands it should at least provide a list of places to play that won't rip you off, that offer a good atmosphere and the kind of audience that your music deserves. For fans I hope it will encourage the occasional trip out to one of the many small venues putting on a whole night of great new bands for £3 or £4.

Things change, as I said, and if you know of any mistakes, or of a venue that should be included in future editions you're more than welcome to get in touch via rocklondon2006@hotmail.co.uk. But, right now, at this particular point in the twenty first century, this is Rock London...The Definitive Guide.

THE VENUES

12 BAR CLUB
ADDRESS: 12 Bar Club, Denmark Street, WC2H 8NL
PHONE: 020 7916 6989 (office) 020 7209 2248 (tickets)
PROMOTER: Andy Lowe
DOOR PRICE: usually £5-£6 (£1 off with flyer)
PRICE OF THEIR MOST POPULAR PINT OR BOTTLE:
£2.95 (pint of Kronenbourg)
OPENING HOURS: Café opens 9.00am till midnight. Bar opens at 11.00am. Music venue opens 7.30pm – 1.00am (Mon – Thurs), 7.30pm – 3.00am (Fri – Sat) 7.00pm – 12.30am (Sun).
FOUNDED: 1994, under this name, 80s as a music venue, 1635 as a forge.
CAPACITY: 150 including café area.
SOME ACTS WHO'VE PLAYED HERE: Coldplay (in '97), Keane, Kathryn Williams, Martha Wainright, Lisa Miskovsky, Bert Jansch, Katie Melua, Jeff Buckley, Turin Brakes.
WHAT'S ON? Four bands a night, seven nights a week playing anything from the leftfields of indie, rock, electro, hip-hop, folk and punk. Clubs include: London Callin' (art-punk, last Sat of month), Blang (anti-folk night), Club Clear (singer-songwriters), occasional open mic nights (see website for further details).
WHAT'S THE SOUND LIKE? Good.
WHO SHOULD BANDS TALK TO ABOUT PLAYING? Send demos to Andy Lowe at the address above specifying if you want to play a particular club night.
WHAT'S THE DEAL FOR BANDS? Bands usually get £1.50 for each person they bring as long as they bring more than 20 people. £2 for

every person if they bring more than 40 but it varies depending on the promoter.

HOW DO WE GET THERE? Nearest tube station is Tottenham Court Road, just round the corner. Take the Charing Cross exit and Denmark Street is about 40 feet down Charing Cross Road on the left.
website: www.12barclub.com

Despite its low ceilings and cramped corners the 12 Bar Club is one of the few venues that really does have 'character'. The original building's been here since 1635 and it feels like it's been very slowly and randomly expanding ever since. One part of it used to be a leper hospital and behind the kitchens there's the start of a blocked off tunnel where they used to take the bodies across the street to the crypt in St Giles' Church. Even before that it housed a forge which was operational right up until the Second World War but, in the 60s, the street it's on became known as London's Tin Pan Alley for the number of music publishing companies and then instrument shops that sprang up here. In the 80s the proprietor of the guitar shop next door decided he needed somewhere for the frustrated musicians on his staff to get over having to listen to guitarists mangling 'Stairway To Heaven' a dozen times a day so he bought it up and turned it into 'The Forge Folk & Blues Club'. Since becoming the 12 Bar Club in 1994 it's become the kind of place that can punch above its weight, hosting showcases for the kind of acts that expect to fill much bigger venues but they still provide a space for unsigned singer-songwriters etc.

93 FEET EAST
ADDRESS: Truman Brewery, 150 Brick Lane, E1 6QN
PHONE: 020 7247 3293
PROMOTER: Sean Hitchings (runs 93Live)
DOOR PRICE: free Mondays, from £4 - £15 in the week depending on the band, free before 9pm on Saturdays £5 afterwards.

93 Feet East - a view of the courtyard

PRICE OF THEIR MOST POPULAR PINT OR BOTTLE:
£3.30 (pint of Grolsch)
OPENING HOURS: 5.00pm – 11.00pm (Mon – Thurs) 5.00pm – 1.00am (Fri) 12.00pm – 1.00am (Sat) 12.00pm – 10.30pm (Sun).
FOUNDED: 2000
CAPACITY: 300 (in the main room) 600 (overall).
SOME ACTS WHO'VE PLAYED HERE: Yeah Yeah Yeahs, Radio 4, The Thrills, Interpol, Bloc Party, Kaiser Chiefs, White Stripes.
WHAT'S ON? Unsigned bands (Mon); a mix of bigger acts and new bands (Tues / Weds / Thurs). Weekends are more clubbing orientated but they still put on live acts. Sundays they show short films with bands

93 Feet East

playing afterwards. Check website for details.
WHAT'S THE SOUND LIKE? Good.
WHO SHOULD BANDS TALK TO ABOUT PLAYING? Send demos to Sean Hitchings at the address above or contact him at Sean@93feeteast.co.uk
WHAT'S THE DEAL FOR BANDS? By negotiation.
HOW DO WE GET THERE? The nearest tube is Shoreditch station on the East London line but it's not far from Liverpool Street and Aldgate East stations. From Aldgate East take the Arts Café exit, turn left into Whitechapel Road and immediately left again on to Osbourne Street. Continue into Brick Lane and 93Ft East is about 500 metres on your right.
website: www.93feeteast.co.uk

At the start of the century you couldn't get much cooler than this bit of Brick Lane. With the Vibe Bar on one side of the street and 93 Feet East on the other it was a big part of the Shoreditch bar / club renaissance that, depending on your point of view, either regenerated the area or turned it into ironic haircut hell. Since then it's probably lost a little of the initial buzz. East London's media types now like to drink in 'authentic' pubs with 'authentic' old people in the corner to add character rather than in converted warehouses. It's outsiders who keep the clubs and style bars of the area so busy at weekends. Like Shoreditch as a whole, though, 93 Feet East has responded by turning to live music in a big way. It's much better placed for this than other venues that have made the same decision. The big room may look a bit cold when it's empty, with its ubiquitous 90s-industrial décor, but it's a great size with good sound. The two small rooms are also very 1999 with their squishy black sofas but that's not such a bad thing and, with weekend barbeques in the courtyard, you won't even have to take a chance on one of the dozens of tempting Indian Restaurants on the street outside.

100 CLUB
ADDRESS: 100 Oxford Street, W1D 1LL
PHONE: 020 7636 0933
OWNER: Jeff Horton
DOOR PRICE: usually £7-£8 but can be more for big names
PRICE OF THEIR MOST POPULAR PINT OR BOTTLE:
£3.10 (pint of Stella Artois)
OPENING HOURS: varies depending on the night but it's usually 7.30pm to around midnight in the week and on Sundays, later on Saturdays.
FOUNDED: 1942 as The Feldman Club (named the 100 Club in 1964)
CAPACITY: 300
SOME ACTS WHO'VE PLAYED HERE: Glen Miller, Muddy Waters, Rolling Stones, The Yardbirds, Sex Pistols, Roxy Music, The Kinks, The Who, The Clash, The Animals, Oasis, White Stripes.
WHAT'S ON? New, cool indie bands midweek (Tues, Weds, Thurs) old chaps playing blues and dusty psychedelia (Fridays), jazz, swing and early

rock'n'roll (Sat), Americana + a Ska club once a month (Sun) jump, jive and swing with dance lessons for beginners (Mon). Check website for updates.

WHAT'S THE SOUND LIKE? Good.

WHO SHOULD BANDS TALK TO ABOUT PLAYING? Most bands are booked by the big promoters, the management don't listen to demos.

WHAT'S THE DEAL FOR BANDS? Depends on the promoter.

HOW DO WE GET THERE? The nearest tube is Tottenham Court Road. Turn left from the Oxford Street exit, cross over the road and it's about 100 yards down.

website: www.the100club.co.uk

In the mid 60s there were over 100 music venues in the West End of London but a combination of market forces and Westminster Council's unfriendly attitude has seen most of them close. Even the 100 Club has struggled at times. In 1976 the place was in the doldrums and it was the decision to be one of the few venues brave enough to put on punk that saved the day. In the 90s the place started to struggle again and this time they were saved by the emergence of unashamedly retro bands like Oasis who relished the chance of standing on the stage where The Pistols and The Stones once played. Recently they've had more problems as new neighbours, who apparently hadn't noticed that they'd moved in near a 63-year-old music venue on Britain's most crowded street, complained about the noise and forced them to give up their late licence on weekdays. But a club that survived the Second World War with the slogan: "Forget the Doodlebug - Come and Jitterbug At the Feldman Club" should be able to survive anything. If you were designing a venue from scratch you probably wouldn't site it on Oxford Street and it wouldn't be this shape (long and narrow like a kind of rock'n'roll corridor) but the 100 Club is deservedly an institution.

ACE CAFE LONDON

ADDRESS: Ace Corner, North Circular Road, Stonebridge, NW10 7UD
PHONE: 020 8961 1000
OWNER: Mark Wilsmore
DOOR PRICE: The café's free, as are some midweek music nights, otherwise prices range from £5-£12.
PRICE OF THEIR MOST POPULAR PINT OR BOTTLE: £2.95 (pint of Stella) (coffee / tea 95p)
OPENING HOURS: 7.00am to 11.00pm (weekdays) 7.00am to 2.00am (Saturdays) 7.00am to 10.30pm (Sundays).
FOUNDED: 1938 originally, then closed in 1969, reopened in 2001
CAPACITY: 360 (inside).
SOME ACTS WHO'VE PLAYED HERE: Ex-Formula One driver Damon Hill's band, 5-6-7-8's, Bad Manners, Rock Bitch.
WHAT'S ON? All kinds of car and bike meets supplemented with various rock'n'roll and rockabilly nights (new bands and original rockers) plus various flavours of Mod, Ska, country, bluegrass and R&B. They've also occasionally had Tim Westwood hosted, 'Pimp My Ride' style hip-hop nights. Check website for details.
WHAT'S THE SOUND LIKE? OK
WHO SHOULD BANDS TALK TO ABOUT PLAYING? Send demos and promo material to Kitty Valentine at the address above.
WHAT'S THE DEAL FOR BANDS? Negotiable, some bands play for beer money in the week, when there's no entrance fee, otherwise it depends on the night.
HOW DO WE GET THERE? If you're coming by public transport the nearest station is Stonebridge Park Station. Turn right and walk down to the North Circular Road, then right again, along the old North Circular Road. The Ace is 100 yards on your right. But nobody would come by public transport, would they? Check website for detailed directions.
website: www.ace-cafe-london.com

Ace Cafe is very different to all the other venues in this book in that its patrons spend much of their time outside in the carpark admiring each other's chrome. When the original café opened in 1938 it was designed to serve the hauliers working the newly built North Circular Road. But, by the early 50s, it was starting to become a favourite of young bikers and, by the time rock'n'roll came along, it was as much a part of the scene as leather jackets, Teddy Boys and tabloid hysteria. The café attracted an awful lot of the latter courtesy of the 'Ton-Up' boys who came to listen to the jukebox and, occasionally, race each other to a given point and back before the record had finished. It became so celebrated that the likes of Gene Vincent would make it a stop-off on their tours from The States. It closed in 1969 as the fashion at the time for turning on, tuning in and dropping out wasn't really compatible with racing at a hundred miles an hour. But, in 1994, a reunion was so successful (12000 bikers turned up) that it was only a matter of time until it reopened. These days there's inevitably an element of nostalgia, with the pot-bellied blokes who used to be the leather-jacketed young dudes still coming along, but they've also made a name for themselves among a whole new generation of petrol-heads.

AIN'T NOTHING BUT BLUES BAR

ADDRESS: 20 Kingly Street, W1B 5P
PHONE: 020 7287 0514
MANAGER: n/a
DOOR PRICE: free in the week and before 8.30 at weekends. £5 after that.
PRICE OF THEIR MOST POPULAR PINT OR BOTTLE:
£3.15 (pint of Stella Artois)
OPENING HOURS: 7.30pm – 12.00am (Sun) 6pm – 1.00am (Mon – Weds) 6.00pm – 2.00am (Thurs) 12.00pm – 3.00am (Fri – Sat).
FOUNDED: 1993
CAPACITY: about 80.

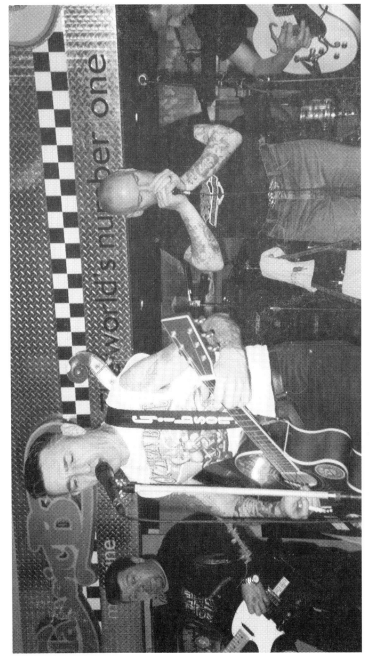

Ace Cafe London

Rock London 2006

SOME ACTS WHO'VE PLAYED HERE: Big Bill Morganfield, Hucklebuck, Barcodes, Dr. Blue & The Prescription.
WHAT'S ON? Saturdays there's an open mic spot from 2.00pm onwards where anyone can turn up. The rest of the time there are various musicians seven nights a week from about 8.00pm onwards. Check website for details.
WHAT'S THE SOUND LIKE? Fine.
WHO SHOULD BANDS TALK TO ABOUT PLAYING? It's probably best to turn up and ask to speak to the manager or come along to the open mic slots on Saturday afternoon.
WHAT'S THE DEAL FOR BANDS? negotiable.
HOW DO WE GET THERE? The nearest tube is Oxford Circus. Take the Regent's Street exit and walk towards Piccadilly, turn left down Great Marlborough Street and then immediately right on to Kingly Street and it's about half way down on the left.
website: www.aintnothinbut.co.uk

Despite their impressively confrontational moniker the Blues Bar do put on musicians who stray from the sacred path of the blues. Not very far, mind, and usually only at their Saturday afternoon open mic slot but the stage of this much loved Soho venue is open to all kinds of guitar strummers as long as they're not expecting to be able to swing a cat or anything much larger than a battered six-string. It's so small that if anyone one turns up with more than about four or five of their mates it will feel full, but that's part of the charm of a place that doesn't feel like it belongs so near to the tacky commercialism of Oxford Circus. There are posters of blues legends all over the walls and, although punters from all over the world come in, they all get to feel like part of a comfortably inclusive clique. Kingly Street has recently undergone a serious makeover, with a big shopping mall awkwardly stuck on one side but it's still a lot nicer than the tacky pseudo-60s tourist trap Carnaby Street, which it runs parallel with, and the Blues Bar is very much a part of that.

ALEXANDRA PALACE

ADDRESS: Alexandra Palace, Alexandra Palace Way, Wood Green, London, N22 7AY
PHONE: 020 8365 2121
MANAGER: Keith Holder
DOOR PRICE: varies, up to about £30
PRICE OF THEIR MOST POPULAR PINT OR BOTTLE: £2.40 (pint of Carlsberg)
OPENING HOURS: varies, check website for details.
FOUNDED: 1873
CAPACITY: 7,250
SOME ACTS WHO'VE PLAYED HERE: The Strokes, The Streets, Razorlight, Faithless, Pink Floyd, Marilyn Manson, Travis, Barry Manilow, Kasabian.
WHAT'S ON? Exhibitions of all kinds plus big bands that like their fans too much to play Wembley but not enough to play three nights at Brixton Academy.
WHAT'S THE SOUND LIKE? Depends on PA brought by the band but the acoustics aren't great.
WHO SHOULD BANDS TALK TO ABOUT PLAYING? n/a
WHAT'S THE DEAL FOR BANDS? n/a
HOW DO WE GET THERE? It has its own mainline train station (11 minutes from King's Cross), or you can get the W3 bus from nearby Wood Green tube or there's a huge carpark with 2,000 spaces.
website: www.alexandrapalace.com

Alexandra Palace has a little more atmosphere than other similarly enormous arena venues if only because the entrance hall is so impressive and it's sited on the top of a hill far above the rest of London, but the experience of watching a band there isn't that much different. It was designed as 'The People's Palace' and it's a nice place to go in the

Alexandra Palace Palm Court

summer when you can appreciate the view from the slightly tacky but ornate Phoenix Bar, the pseudo-classical Victorian architecture, the park and boating lake outside. When bands play, though, none of this is particularly noticeable. Instead it's just another cavernous hall designed to squeeze as many people in as possible and, as always, some bands can play and make it throb like a club gig others rattle emptily in the big hall. If it's a choice between here or Wembley then you'd probably hope your favourite band come here but there's not much in it. Both of them are a long way from the centre of town and neither of them were designed with acoustics as a consideration.

Travis at the Alexandra Palace

AMERSHAM ARMS
ADDRESS: 388 New Cross Road, New Cross, London, SE14 6TY
PHONE: 0208 692 2047 (pub) 020 8690 8980 (promoter)
PROMOTER: Titch Turner
DOOR PRICE: usually £5 (£4 with a flyer). £3 for Glue Rooms
PRICE OF THEIR MOST POPULAR PINT OR BOTTLE:
£2.60 (pint of Carling)
OPENING HOURS: 8.30pm – midnight (Sun – Weds) 8.30pm - 2.00am (Thurs – Sat)
FOUNDED: 1904 as the Amersham Hotel

Alexandra Palace - Palm Court Centre

CAPACITY: about 200

SOME ACTS WHO'VE PLAYED HERE: Chas & Dave, Wreckless Eric, Sepultura, Suede, Wilko Johnson.

WHAT'S ON? Roots / Jazz (Tues), Jazz (Thurs) new bands (Fri / Sat) comedy (alternate Monday) occasional bands other nights. Plus the famously odd art-music night Glue Rooms on the last Weds of every month.

WHAT'S THE SOUND LIKE? Pretty good.

WHO SHOULD BANDS TALK TO ABOUT PLAYING? Send demos to Titch Turner at the address above.

WHAT'S THE DEAL FOR BANDS? Negotiable.

HOW DO WE GET THERE? From New Cross tube station turn right and it's just down the road on the left.

website: www.catapultclub.co.uk

If you come to the Amersham Arms looking for the famously vibrant New Cross scene you're likely to be a bit disappointed. It's the first pub you'll see as you turn right out of New Cross station and it doesn't exactly radiate rock'n'roll excitement. The pub bit is nice enough in a gentle, long-term alcoholism kind of way, but the club bit next door seems to be aiming at a more mature audience than most of the young and cool venues in the area. There are too many tables for it to work as a raucous rock venue and yet it's not fancy enough to carry off its slightly suburban attempt at sophistication. However, if you come to New Cross and find yourself horribly intimidated by the art students down at the Six String Bar or The Montague Arms then this might be a more congenial environment. Apart from the Glue Rooms night (see above) they seem to go for more mature, sensible acts and a more mature audience. As a selling point 'come here if you're too old or too ugly for the Six String' might not be particularly ringing but there's certainly a gap in the market.

ARCHWAY TAVERN

ADDRESS: Archway Tavern, 1 Archway Close, Upper Holloway N19 3TX

PHONE: 020 7272 2840

OWNER: Patrick O'Neill

DOOR PRICE: usually around £5 (£3 students / £4.50 with flyer)

PRICE OF THEIR MOST POPULAR PINT OR BOTTLE: £2.80 (pint of Stella Artois)

OPENING HOURS: 11.00am – 1.00am (Sun - Weds) (11.00am- 2.30am Thurs - Sat)

FOUNDED: 1813 as a pub, 1960s as a music venue

CAPACITY: 260

SOME ACTS WHO'VE PLAYED HERE: The Kinks, The Dubliners, The Wolftones.

WHAT'S ON? New bands on Mondays and Thursdays, tribute or covers bands on Saturdays.

WHAT'S THE SOUND LIKE? Not great although there is talk of improvements.

WHO SHOULD BANDS TALK TO ABOUT PLAYING? Send demos to Irene at the address above.

WHAT'S THE DEAL FOR BANDS? Monday nights they get 50% of the door after the first 20 people they bring. Check with promoter for other nights.

HOW DO WE GET THERE? It's directly opposite Archway Tube Station, take the exit on the right as you leave the station.

website: none.

The Archway Tavern is best known as "the home of The Kinks". They signed their first record contract here and they were pictured propping up the bar on the cover of their 1971 album 'Muswell Hillbillies'. Apparently Ray Davies used to come here with his family and listen to "the worst country and western album in the world". Anyone who's been in to see a band since then would be tempted to observe that not much has changed. They keep talking about turning the big, slightly bland room next to the pub into a proper music venue (there's a sign outside ludicrously claiming that it's "North London's premier music venue") but so far not much seems to be happening. If they can persuade bands and fans up the two stops on the tube from Camden it could work because the Archway isn't a bad pub despite its slightly bizarre travel-themed furnishings (a toy tram runs along a beam by the ceiling in the saloon bar). Maybe the place doesn't have quite such an 'indie' atmosphere as, say, the Bull & Gate but there's an opportunity here if bands or promoters want to take it.

THE ASTORIA

ADDRESS: 157 Charing Cross Road, WC2H 0EL.
PHONE: 020 7434 9592
MANAGER: Mark Ellicot
DOOR PRICE: Varies between £7-£25 depending on the band.
PRICE OF THEIR MOST POPULAR PINT OR BOTTLE:
£3.10 for a can of Grolsch.
OPENING HOURS: usually about 6.30pm – 10.30pm (when the G-A-Y club is on afterwards) or 7.00pm – 11.00pm when it's not.
FOUNDED: About 20 years ago as a music venue but the building's been here since the nineteenth century and it's had various occupants.
CAPACITY: 2000
SOME ACTS WHO'VE PLAYED HERE: U2, Nirvana, Blur, The White Stripes – too many to mention. Most credible rock bands of the last 20 years have played.
WHAT'S ON? Major touring bands seven nights a week. After gigs on Mondays, Thursdays, Fridays and Saturdays they kick everyone out early to host the famous G-A-Y club which has seen PAs from the likes of Atomic Kitten and Kylie.

Rock London 2006

WHAT'S THE SOUND LIKE? Excellent
WHO SHOULD BANDS TALK TO ABOUT PLAYING? All done through promoters.
WHAT'S THE DEAL FOR BANDS? n/a
HOW DO WE GET THERE? It's just round the corner from Tottenham Court Road tube station on Charing Cross Road (follow the signs from the station). It's also on the main bus route for many buses that terminate at the nearby Trafalgar Square.
website: www.meanfiddler.com

The Astoria started life as a factory for Cross And Blackwell and since then it's had stints as a music hall, strip club and a cinema. Its latest incarnation probably suits it best, though, if only because rock fans are less fussy than pickle manufacturers and erotic dancers about cleanliness and nice décor. From the outside it still has an air of faded grandeur but inside the grandeur has not so much faded as been entirely covered by a thick layer of sweat, cigarette smoke and lager vapours. There's a seated area upstairs which is grimier but also more atmospheric than a lot of venues' standing areas and, as the tickets aren't restricted, you can still head downstairs to where the action is. There's no nonchalant leaning on the bar here (partly because at least one bar's about seven feet high and even reaching up for a can of over-priced lager makes you feel like a small child buying an ice-cream) but also because the ambience is far too rock'n'roll. There have been rumours that the new Crossrail project may involve demolishing the whole corner of Charing Cross Road, Oxford Street and Tottenham Court Road. Such attempts should be resisted because The Astoria is part of London's rock scenery and the fact that the interior is half gothic mansion, half provincial bus shelter only adds to its charm.

BARBICAN CENTRE

ADDRESS: Barbican Centre, Silk Street, EC2Y 8DS
PHONE: 020 7638 4141
MANAGING DIRECTOR: John Tusa
DOOR PRICE: For live music prices range from £12.50 - £35
PRICE OF THEIR MOST POPULAR PINT OR BOTTLE: £2.95 (bottle of Becks or Budvar)
OPENING HOURS: 9.00am – 11.00pm (Mon – Sat) 12.00pm – 11.00pm (Sun and Public Holidays)
FOUNDED: 1982
CAPACITY: 2000 in the main auditorium
SOME ACTS WHO'VE PLAYED HERE: Lou Reed, Asian Dub Foundation (providing a new score for French film 'La Haine'), Lambchop, Herbie Hancock, Death In Vegas.
WHAT'S ON? A huge range of arts, cinema, classical music, jazz, folk rock, dance, theatre, etc etc. Check website for details.
WHAT'S THE SOUND LIKE? Excellent
WHO SHOULD BANDS TALK TO ABOUT PLAYING? They tend not to put bands on unless there's some kind of gimmick, sorry 'theme', involved such as April 2005's 'It Came From Memphis' featuring a whole range of music that came from, erm, Memphis.
WHAT'S THE DEAL FOR BANDS? n/a
HOW DO WE GET THERE? Nearest tube station is Barbican. From there cross Aldersgate Street. Walk through the road tunnel (Beech Street) before taking the first turning right into Silk Street. The Barbican is straight ahead. Moorgate, St Paul's, Bank, Liverpool Street and Mansion House stations are also nearby.
website: www.barbican.org.uk

The Barbican was first planned shortly after World War II when bombing had devastated the whole area. The architects envisioned a new way of living with an arts centre plonked right in the middle of a housing estate. Even after the more expensive bits of the plans were ditched, such as walkways in the sky, (50s architects were obsessed with walkways in the sky) it still took until the 70s for construction to get going and it was finally completed in 1982 at a cost of over £400 million at today's prices. The Arts Centre itself is mostly underground with live music of all kinds in an extremely plush 2000-seater concert hall but there are also three cinemas, three art galleries and a 1000 seater theatre. The result is probably more middle class than the architects' intention (the flats around the centre go for a fortune) but the Barbican are the third largest funder of the arts in Britain so for the music bookers it must be like fantasy promotion. If they decide they want to have a month of Mexican country or a fortnight of Glaswegian drum'n'bass then chances are they'll get it.

BARDEN'S BOUDOIR

Address: 38-44 Stoke Newington Road, N16 7XJ
Phone: n/a
Promoter: Andrew Doig
Door price: £3 - £5
Price of their most popular pint or bottle:
£2.80 (pint of Kronenbourg)
Opening hours: 8.00pm – 1.00am (later at weekends). Only open when events are booked.
Founded: January 2005
Capacity: 350
Some acts who've played here: Prefuse 73, Clor, The Broken Family Band, Four Tet.
What's on? Electronica, hardcore, punk, metal, indie, etc
What's the sound like? OK
Who should bands talk to about playing? Send demos to Andrew Doig at the address above.
What's the deal for bands? All bands get paid by negotiation

according to how much is in the till.

HOW DO WE GET THERE? The nearest station is Dalston-Kingsland mainline (five minutes by train from Highbury and Islington). Turn left out of the station and it's five minutes walk on the right. Details of bus routes and a map are on the website.

website: www.bardensbar.co.uk

When they said that brand new venue Barden's Boudoir was in the basement of a closed furniture shop I was expecting something a bit more gritty and urban with maybe a few token scarlet cushions strewn around in a nod to the 'Boudoir' theme. Instead, when you get down there there's something strangely domestic about the place. The bar looks like it's been stolen from a mid-priced country hotel and, when it's half empty, which is probably most of the time considering the large capacity, the acres of empty concrete floor space have the atmosphere of a provincial car park. Apart from a few sad booths very little effort has gone on internal décor and yet it doesn't have the edginess that you'd expect from what is basically a legal squat. Still, there's something heroic about the attempt to turn something so seemingly inappropriate into a rock club. The promoters have already managed to draw some interesting new bands down here and, although Stoke Newington isn't the easiest place to get to for outsiders, (no tube line) for £3-£4 it might be worth the trip.

THE BARFLY

ADDRESS: 49 Chalk Farm Road, NW1 8AN
PHONE: 0870 9070999 (tickets) 0207 691 4244 (office)
MANAGER: Jeremy Ledlin and Michael Nicholas
DOOR PRICE: £3 - £12
PRICE OF THEIR MOST POPULAR PINT OR BOTTLE:
£2.90 (pint of Grolsch)
OPENING HOURS: usually 6.30pm – 11.00pm but it's open till 2.00am

on Fridays and Saturdays.

FOUNDED: Barfly started at another Camden pub, The Falcon, in 1996 although there were occasional gigs at these premises when it was just The Monarch. Barfly moved here in 2000.

CAPACITY: 200 upstairs in the venue, 200 downstairs in the bar.

SOME ACTS WHO'VE PLAYED HERE: The Strokes, The Darkness, The Cure, Death in Vegas, Feeder, Badly Drawn Boy, Coldplay, Muse, Doves.

WHAT'S ON? Four bands a night, seven nights a week plus clubs afterwards Queens of Noise (Fridays) for trashy indie, rock, soul and more bands. Transmission (every fourth Saturday) dancey guitars, beats and funk. Kill 'Em All Let God Sort It Out (Alternate Saturdays) electro and rock. Casino Royale (every fourth Saturday) hi-class indie disco plus northern soul and psychedelia. Check website for updates and more details.

WHAT'S THE SOUND LIKE? Good.

WHO SHOULD BANDS TALK TO ABOUT PLAYING? Send demos

to Barfly Bookings, 59-61 Farringdon Road, London, EC1M 3JB
WHAT'S THE DEAL FOR BANDS? For small bands the first ten people they bring cover the costs and after that they get a percentage of the door. For larger bands it's negotiable.
HOW DO WE GET THERE? The nearest tube station is Chalk Farm. Turn left out of the tube, at the junction shortly after turn right onto the main road and continue along Chalk Farm Road for 250 metres. Barfly is on the left side on the corner of Ferdinand Street and Chalk Farm Road. From Camden tube it's about five minutes walk. Turn right up Camden High Street and it eventually turns into Chalk Farm Road.
website: www.barflyclub.com

Most people who go to gigs regularly in London have a love / hate relationship with Camden. It's dirty and crowded and there are a fair few mad, scary or just plain annoying people around but it also has some of the best music you'll hear anywhere. The same goes several times over for The Barfly. Although it's nearer Chalk Farm Station than Camden Station it's got a fair claim to be the pumping black heart of the area's music scene. Downstairs in the relatively pleasant pub there are posters all over the wall with the names of the bands who are about to play and almost all of them probably felt they were that bit closer to 'making it' after appearing there for the first time. This is partly because there are often more industry people in the crowd than there are regular punters and, although on nights like this the atmosphere can be slightly weird (sort of a cross between an auction, a public execution and a zoo), this only increases the urgency of up-and-coming bands' desire to play. There are many things not to like about the place, not least the sweltering heat in the summer (and the winter, come to think of it) and the manky toilets, but the fact that 'Barfly' is now an empire with its own free magazine, student radio station and a chain of venues across the country, suggests they must be doing something right.

THE BEDFORD

ADDRESS: 77 Bedford Hill, Balham, SW12 9HD
PHONE: 020 8682 8940
MANAGER (music): Tony Moore
DOOR PRICE: free (for music, check website or listings for comedy)
PRICE OF THEIR MOST POPULAR PINT OR BOTTLE:
£2.90 (pint of Stella)
OPENING HOURS: 10.30am – 11.00pm (Sun – Weds) 10.30am – midnight (Thurs) 10.30am – 2.00am (Fri – Sat)
FOUNDED: 150 – 200 years ago.
CAPACITY: 250 (main room)
SOME ACTS WHO'VE PLAYED HERE: The Finn Brothers, The Rolling Stones (Possibly. Some regulars claim they played here in their early days) The Lighthouse Family, KT Tunstall.
WHAT'S ON? Live music every night of the week except Friday and Saturday when the comedy and disco takes over. Plus dance classes etc (check website for details).
WHAT'S THE SOUND LIKE? OK for the singer-songwriter / solo artist type stuff they tend to put on.
WHO SHOULD BANDS TALK TO ABOUT PLAYING? Send demos in the house style (see website for details) to The Booking Team at the address above.
WHAT'S THE DEAL FOR BANDS? There's no door charge, bands generally play for the love of it.
HOW DO WE GET THERE? Nearest tube is Balham. Check website for map and directions.
website: www.thebedford.co.uk

The Bedford like to refer to the vibe at their music nights as being similar to the 'Later With Jules Holland' programme on BBC2. This means, essentially, that the vibe is pretty, erm, mature but also that, rather than playing whole 'sets' musicians play a couple of songs each,

The Bedford by night

taking it in turns to use the house equipment. Whether you think this is a good thing or bad thing probably depends on whether you are someone who's in the habit of staying in on Friday nights to watch Jules. It's all very civilised and it's not hard to see why the likes of the Finn Brothers and the Lighthouse Family have called in. It might not be to everybody's taste but you have to remember that this is the pub that, with its 'Balham Banana' comedy nights, has rivalled the West End for picking up on new stand-up talent for the last twenty years, long before most people would have even considered heading down to this part of town. Balham is essentially a less pretentious version of Clapham and The Bedford is a small part of the reason why people down there claim to like the place.

BETSEY TROTWOOD

ADDRESS: 56 Farringdon Road, EC1R 3BL
PHONE: 020 7253 4285 (pub) 020 7336 7326 (promoters)
PROMOTERS: Sarah and Matthew at Plum Promotions
DOOR PRICE: £5 (£4 students)
PRICE OF THEIR MOST POPULAR PINT OR BOTTLE: £2.70 (pint of Stella Artois)
OPENING HOURS: Pub's open from 12.00pm. Bands normally on 7.30pm – 11.00pm.
FOUNDED: 2002 as a music venue.
CAPACITY: 60
SOME ACTS WHO'VE PLAYED HERE: Keane, Bernard Butler, Simple Kid, Tompaulin, Magic Numbers, House Of Love.
WHAT'S ON? Bands most nights plus Plug And Play (electro – 1st Friday every month); Shock Therapy (punk, noise etc – last Friday every month). Plus comedy upstairs.
WHAT'S THE SOUND LIKE? OK
WHO SHOULD BANDS TALK TO ABOUT PLAYING? Send demos to Sarah, Matthew, Plum Promotions at the address above

WHAT'S THE DEAL FOR BANDS? By negotiation but usually need to bring people to get paid.
HOW DO WE GET THERE? Nearest tube is Farringdon. Turn right out of the station and then right again when you get to Farringdon Road. The Betsey Trotwood is about half a mile down on your right.
website: www.plumpromotions.co.uk (promoters)

It's traditional to say that seeing bands in a very small venue is "like seeing them in your front room". This would usually only be the case if your front room was in a particularly insalubrious crack house frequented by people who piss cheap lager over your carpets. At the Betsey Trotwood, though, the cliché has some validity – the basement is every bit as cosy and intimate as the name suggests. The pub, named after a character in 'David Copperfield', has been here for years and is frequented by a mixture of journalists from The Guardian (over the road) and other local media and city types. When Plum Promotions (who also book bands for the Water Rats and the Marquee) started putting on bands here they seemed initially to mostly go for acts who fulfil the same, friendly living room vibe. Since then there have been the odd appearance from noisier bands but the vibe is still very laidback and relaxed. Farringdon has become ruthlessly cool over the last ten years, with an intimidating mixture of City money and Hoxton bar culture, but the Betsey Trotwood remains incongruously indie, low-key and self-effacing.

BLOOMSBURY THEATRE
(The UCL Bloomsbury)
ADDRESS: 15 Gordon Street, WC1H 0AH
PHONE: 020 7388 8822
MANAGER: Peter Cadley
DOOR PRICE: varies (from £10 - £25)
PRICE OF THEIR MOST POPULAR PINT OR BOTTLE:

£3 (bottle of Kronenbourg)
OPENING HOURS: varies (usually about 7.00pm-11.00pm)
FOUNDED: 1968 as The Collegiate Theatre. In 1982 it became The Bloomsbury Theatre and in 2001 it became The UCL Bloomsbury.
CAPACITY: 558 Seated 35 standing
SOME ACTS WHO'VE PLAYED HERE: Tindersticks, The Rutles, Lily Savage, Eddie Izzard, Sooty.
WHAT'S ON? Usually bands about once a month and a variety of theatre, comedy etc. Check website for details.
WHAT'S THE SOUND LIKE? Excellent
WHO SHOULD BANDS TALK TO ABOUT PLAYING? All booked through promoters.
WHAT'S THE DEAL FOR BANDS? n/a
HOW DO WE GET THERE? The nearest tube is Euston Square (turn left down Gower Place when you come out of the station and Gordon Street is a little way down on the right). It's also near Warren Street, Euston and Euston mainline station.
website: www.thebloomsbury.com

The Bloomsbury Theatre isn't exactly a rock venue. For twelve weeks a year it plays host to the University College London's forays into proper theatre and the rest of the time it's hired out to the whole rag-bag of what we could loosely call 'showbiz', from comedians like Eddie Izzard to 'Wind In The Willows'. Every now and then, though, they let in a band who either have pretensions to a certain sophistication that suits the plush seats and comfortable environment, or else who have a fanbase that are getting on a bit and need a nice sit down. If you look closely, Bloomsbury Theatre is nowhere near as grand or aesthetically pleasing as much more 'rock' venues like the Brixton Academy but it does have a kind of discreet, unshowy sophistication. Compared with most crap-holes owned by universities, of course, it could be the Taj Mahal. The seating is comfortable and roomy, service at the bar is pretty quick and if you want to hear the place at its best you can probably still buy 'The Tindersticks Live At Bloomsbury Theatre' at which the gloomy ones make full use of the stately goth vibe and impressive acoustics.

THE BOOGALOO
Address: 312 Archway Road, Highgate, N6
Phone: 020 8340 2928
Promoter: Gerry O'Boyle
Door price: usually free until 10.30pm (£5 afterwards)
Price of their most popular pint or bottle: £2.90 (Stella Artois)
Opening hours: 5.30pm – 11.00pm (Sun-Weds) 5.30pm – 12.30pm (Thurs) 5.30pm – 1.30am (Fri-Sat)
Founded: 2002 as the Boogaloo
Capacity: 160
Some acts who've played here: Bright Eyes, The Pogues, Yeti, Pete Doherty, Youth Group. Coldplay when it was called The Shepherd's.
What's on? Unsigned bands first Monday of every month, occasional appearances from bigger names, music quiz 'You're Gonna Need A Bigger Boat', hip literary readings night 'Vox'n'Roll at regular intervals (check website for details).
What's the sound like? OK
Who should bands talk to about playing? Turn up on new bands night (first Monday of the month) and register with Anna Page.
What's the deal for bands? By negotiation.
How do we get there? It's virtually next door to Highgate tube station on the corner of Shepherd's Hill.
website: www.boogaloo.org

Before it became The Boogaloo this Highgate pub used to be called The

Shepherd's and it was the kind of place that certain locals built their life around. To get an idea of what it was like you only need to watch 'Shaun Of The Dead'. The zombie comedy's stars Simon Pegg and Nick Frost spent much of their twenties here. Because of its history, then, there was a lot of suspicion when the current owners of the Boogaloo came in with their ideas for a new "theme pub" and started ripping the beer-sodden carpet up. To most British drinkers the words "pub" and "theme" are about as welcome next to each other as "sexually" and "transmitted disease". Fortunately The Boogaloo's 'theme' was to reinvent the idea of a 'Juke Joint' where the jukebox, instead of being a forgotten money-sucker in the corner, is the centrepiece. The well-connected landlords got various musicians and others to fill it with their favourite records and it's been a curious mixture of local pub and indie 'celeb' hang-out ever since. It doesn't really work as a venue, the stage looks awkward and out of place halfway down one wall but, despite this, the pub's pulling power means you never know who'll be playing.

THE BORDERLINE

Address: Orange Yard, Manette Street W1D 4JB
Phone: 020 7734 5547
Promoter: Barry Everitt
Door price: usually £7, depending on night (£5 with support band flyer).
Price of their most popular pint or bottle: £2.65 (pint of Guinness)
Opening hours: 7.00pm – 11.00pm bands (11.00pm - 3.00am for clubs listed below)
Founded: 1989
Capacity: 300
Who's played here? Oasis, REM, Pearl Jam, Blur, Muse, Jeff Buckley, Ryan Adams, Blondie.
What's on? Live music seven nights a week plus late clubs Vanity

(punk / hip-hop / metal – last Mon of the month); Rockit (punk / rock / metal – Thurs); Club Fandango (best of Club Fandango's various London nights every 3rd Thurs 7.00pm-11.00pm) The Queen Is Dead (Alan McGee's indie / etc night – Fri); The Christmas Club (indie / dance – Sat); The Fallen Angel (sophisticated jazz / blues lounge-club 7.00pm-11.00pm Sun)

WHAT'S THE SOUND LIKE? Good.

WHO SHOULD BANDS TALK TO ABOUT PLAYING? Send demos to Barry Everitt, Borderline Promotions, 157 Charing Cross Road, WC2H 0EN)

WHAT'S THE DEAL FOR BANDS? Headline bands need to bring at least 180 people and they're paid 75% of the door after costs. Support bands are offered flyer deal and guaranteed at least £50.

HOW DO WE GET THERE? Nearest tube station is Tottenham Court Road. Turn right down Charing Cross Road and it's at the back of a small courtyard (Orange Yard), which is just past The Astoria on your right. website: www.meanfiddler.com

Most cellar venues have a kind of edgy, underground cool but not The Borderline. You enter it through what looks like a garden shed and once you're inside it's a cosy, gentle kind of place. If you arrive during a quiet bit of a song you can find your arrival down the stairs is more distracting, and more visible for most of the crowd, than whatever's happening on the stage. This is partly because the stage is only about six inches off the ground and partly because if you want to get to the bar you'll have to cut a swathe through the middle of them. Maybe because of this the divide between band and audience seems much thinner than in other, similarly sized, venues. If you watch from a stool at the far end of the bar you'll be roughly level with the drummer's head. This, along with the vaguely TexMex décor (it used to be the cellar for Mexican restaurant Break For The Border), makes for an atmosphere which is ideal for the laidback Americana and country which first made the place's name. They've moved on since then with numerous club nights but, even if you're listening to a DJ playing Slipknot, the cosy, family restaurant feel remains.

BOSTON ARMS
ADDRESS: 178 Junction Road, N19 5QQ
PHONE: 020 7272 8153 (pub)
PROMOTER: Paul Somerville
DOOR PRICE: £6 (£1 off if you join the mailing list)
PRICE OF THEIR MOST POPULAR PINT OR BOTTLE:
£2.80 (pint of Kronenbourg)
OPENING HOURS: 8.30pm - 3.00am
FOUNDED: 1997 (as The Dirty Water Club)
CAPACITY: 150
SOME ACTS WHO'VE PLAYED HERE: The White Stripes, The Datsuns, The Von Bondies, Rocket Science, The Kills, the D4, Goldblade, The Buff Medways.
WHAT'S ON? Garage rock, punk, etc every Friday night
WHAT'S THE SOUND LIKE? Good
WHO SHOULD BANDS TALK TO ABOUT PLAYING? Send demos to the address above (check website for guidelines)
WHAT'S THE DEAL FOR BANDS? By negotiation (no pay to play or deposit)
HOW DO WE GET THERE? It's right opposite Tufnell Park tube station on the Northern Line.
website: www.dirtywaterclub.com

The Boston Arms is a big, ferociously scruffy local pub with furniture that looks like it's been gnawed by fearsome rodents and an ambience which is like a post-apocalyptic social club. That's probably why the founders of The Dirty Water Club decided that Harper's Bar next door would be a good place to put on the kind of music which you could also describe as ferociously scruffy or just plain ferocious. Long before it became fashionable again The Dirty Water Club was one of the places in London to see garage rock, punk and all forms of unadulterated rock'n'roll. The venue's website sternly points out that they don't generally book bands that use drum machines and that purist ethic is probably one reason why The White Stripes and many lesser bands of a similar ilk have beaten a path to its door. It's also thanks to the efforts of artist Wild Billy Childish and his band The Buff Medways who've had a monthly residency here forever, long before bands like The Hives took garage rock to the top of the charts. If the venue was a person it would be Billy and, probably, vice versa.

BRIXTON ACADEMY

(Carling Academy Brixton)
ADDRESS: Brixton Academy, 211 Stockwell Road SW9 9SL
PHONE: 020 7771 3000
MANAGER: Nigel Downs
DOOR PRICE: usually from £12 - £30
PRICE OF THEIR MOST POPULAR PINT OR BOTTLE:
£2.95 (can, bottle or pint of Carling)
OPENING HOURS: bands usually 7.00pm – 11.00pm but they do sometimes open later.
FOUNDED: 1983 as a music venue (built 1929).
CAPACITY: 4,921 (3,300 standing)
SOME ACTS WHO'VE PLAYED HERE: Slipnot, Bob Dylan, Madonna, The Killers, Rolling Stones, Eminem, Prodigy, Radiohead, Iron Maiden, Missy Elliot, The Streets, The Smiths last ever performance.
WHAT'S ON? Big name bands several nights a week.
WHAT'S THE SOUND LIKE? Very variable. Sometimes the vocals seem to get lost in the mix.
WHO SHOULD BANDS TALK TO ABOUT PLAYING? n/a
WHAT'S THE DEAL FOR BANDS? n/a
HOW DO WE GET THERE? From Brixton tube turn right down

Brixton Road under the railway bridge and Stockwell Road is a short way down on the left. Brixton mainline railway station and Stockwell tube are also nearby.
website: www.brixton-academy.co.uk

If it wasn't for Brixton Academy most suburban kids in the 80s and 90s would have got their impression of the area almost exclusively from TV footage of the riot that hit Brixton in 1981. As it is the trip down the Victoria Line has been a rite of passage for thousands and it's been voted as one of the best venues in London in numerous polls. Like Hammersmith Apollo, the Astoria and many other venues of this size it was built in the late twenties as a cinema in the days before cinema builders realised that it was pointless making something that people sit in in the dark look so pretty. Some of the Art Deco plasterwork has been ripped out but it still looks impressive with an arch in front of the stage and, hurrah, a gently sloping floor so even shortarses get a good view from pretty much anywhere. The upstairs seating bit is less impressive so it's worth trying to buy tickets early to get a place downstairs. Ironically one of the venue's unique features rarely gets used. Apparently you can drive straight on to the stage from the street and in 1952 the British winner of the Monte Carlo Rally did just that. Something for The Darkness to think about, perhaps.

BUFFALO BAR
ADDRESS: 259 Upper Street, N1
PHONE: 020 7359 6191
OWNER: Stacey Thomas
DOOR PRICE: about £5 usually, £8 for bigger bands (Artrocker is free to members)
PRICE OF THEIR MOST POPULAR PINT OR BOTTLE:
£2.80 (bottle of Becks)
OPENING HOURS: usually 8.00pm – 2.00am (midnight on Sundays)

FOUNDED: 2001 as the Buffalo Bar.
CAPACITY: 150
SOME ACTS WHO'VE PLAYED HERE: Towers Of London, The Thrills, The Subways, Magic Numbers, Kaito, Futureheads, Oneida, Bloc Party
WHAT'S ON? Indie / rock bands most nights of the week and various club nights (Artrocker – Tues; Goo – Weds; plus too many monthly nights to mention) Check website for details.
WHAT'S THE SOUND LIKE? Good.
WHO SHOULD BANDS TALK TO ABOUT PLAYING? Send demos to the promoter of the night you want to play c/o the Buffalo Bar (see above)
WHAT'S THE DEAL FOR BANDS? Depends on promoter.
HOW DO WE GET THERE? It's right next to Highbury and Islington tube on the Victoria Line, underneath the Famous Cock Tavern.
website: www.buffalobar.co.uk

The emergence of The Buffalo Bar is one of the best things that's happened to London's rock scene in the last few years. Bands played here before when it used to be part of the Po-Na-Na chain but, partly thanks to the Artrocker residency on Tuesday nights, and the other excellent promoters, it's suddenly become an indispensable part of the gig circuit. This is mostly because of the booking policy but the basement venue has a nice intimacy and an underground feel in a metaphorical sense as well as a literal one. The stage is very low and, as in most cellar clubs, there are pillars blocking the view from various angles but having to make a bit of an effort to see isn't as much of a chore as it could be. Even if you do end up spilling your pint over someone the atmosphere's generally good enough that they won't turn around and punch you. Well, not too hard anyway. It's also about ten feet from Highbury and Islington tube, which is very handy. Before becoming a music venue the original owners used it as a wine cellar, an off-license and then a club and the fact that it's most successful incarnation has been showcasing relatively obscure rock bands is very encouraging.

BULL & GATE
ADDRESS: 389 Kentish Town Road, London, NW5 2TJ
PHONE: 020 7093 4820 (promoters)
MANAGER: Phil Avey and Andy Clarke
DOOR PRICE: usually £5
PRICE OF THEIR MOST POPULAR PINT OR BOTTLE: £2.50 (pint of Carling)
OPENING HOURS: usually 8.00pm – 11.15pm. Pub's open till midnight at weekends.
FOUNDED: 1979 as a music venue.
CAPACITY: 150
SOME ACTS WHO'VE PLAYED HERE: PJ Harvey, Carter USM, Senseless Things, Coldplay, Keane, The Darkness, Maximo Park, Ash.
WHAT'S ON? New bands of all different kinds, seven nights a week.
WHAT'S THE SOUND LIKE? OK
WHO SHOULD BANDS TALK TO ABOUT PLAYING? Send demos to: Bull & Gate Promotions, Building A, Trinity Buoy Wharf, 64 Orchard Place, London, E14 0JW (promoters Andy & Phil say they'll still be promoting at other venues even if the worst happens here)
WHAT'S THE DEAL FOR BANDS? 60% of the door after the first 19 people.
HOW DO WE GET THERE? Nearest tube is Kentish Town on the Northern Line. Turn right out of the station and where the road forks keep left. The Bull And Gate is just before The Forum on the left.

The Bull & Gate has been here as a pub since the 17th century and they've been putting on ye olde noisie indie musick for almost as long. Well, since 1979 anyway. It's always occupied a place in the gig circuit somewhere below the fractionally bigger venues a mile down the road in Camden and, as such, has earned a reputation for giving hundreds of bands their first chance. Worryingly, at the time of writing, the owners are about to auction the place (in September 2005) and, as there're no planning restrictions, it could end up as anything from a theme pub to a block of flats. Like all the best venues it's a simple affair with a nice, old-fashioned pub on one side and a grimy, box where the bands play on the other. In between is a bar that serves as a sort of decompression chamber for those moving between the fairly local atmosphere of the pub and the more indie / alternative atmosphere of the venue. If it's still open by the time this book comes out, and with luck it will be, then attending a night without knowing who's on is still a case of lucky dip but it's always worth having a flutter.

BULLET BAR

ADDRESS: 147 Kentish Town Road, Camden, NW1.
PHONE: 020 7485 6040
OWNER: Adam Marshall
DOOR PRICE: £3 on Mondays, £6 for Sand club, £2 for open mic nights, free the rest of the time.
PRICE OF THEIR MOST POPULAR PINT OR BOTTLE:
£3.00 (pint of Kronenbourg)
OPENING HOURS: 6.00pm-midnight (Sun – Weds), 6.00pm-1.00am (Thurs) 6.00pm – 2.00am (Fri – Sat).
FOUNDED: 2004 as Bullet Bar but before that it was The Verge and it was a pub called The Castle for years before that.
CAPACITY: 150
SOME ACTS WHO'VE PLAYED HERE: In The Verge days: Graham Coxon, The Libertines, The Darkness, Keane.
WHAT'S ON? Alternate Sundays it's either the Sand Club (Jazz, Jive and Blues bands), or an open mic night for singer-songwriters. Mondays is new bands.
WHAT'S THE SOUND LIKE? OK.

WHO SHOULD BANDS TALK TO ABOUT PLAYING? Send demos to the address above.
WHAT'S THE DEAL FOR BANDS? Cut of the door (negotiable) no pay to play or deposit.
HOW DO WE GET THERE? It's in between Camden and Kentish Town Tube Stations.
website: www.bulletbar.co.uk

A year or two ago if you stumbled into this pub, when it was still called The Verge, you'd have nothing but a few aging Britpop refugees for company. Next door there's a 'Cash Converters' shop and a massage parlour and you could tell that some of the patrons thought that the chance to flog your stereo and then spend the money on beer and a nice, erm, massage would be pretty much the perfect night (or even day) out. Since then there's been a mini-revolution. The new patrons have totally gutted the place and turned it into what could pass as the bar of an expensive hotel with plush furniture, scarlet walls and fancy cocktails. This is a brave move but maybe a sensible one as the initial scenario was quite unlikely. Nobody just stumbled into The Verge. It was located halfway between Camden and Kentish Town tube stations at exactly the point where the drug dealers of the former start to give way to the muggers and murderers of the latter so the owners had to turn it into the kind of destination bar that people will make an effort to get to. They've kept the old pub's musical heritage alive, just, with The Sand Club and an open mic night on Sundays, although on one of my visits the earnest, but quite talented singer-songwriters, seemed like the least cool people in there amongst the trendy bar types.

BUSH HALL

ADDRESS: 310 Uxbridge Road, London, W12 7LJ
PHONE: 020 8222 6933 (tickets) 020 8222 6955 (office)
PROMOTER: Kath Ratcliffe (music booking)
DOOR PRICE: from £5 (for 'Buzz Nights') up to about £17.50
PRICE OF THEIR MOST POPULAR PINT OR BOTTLE:
£3 (bottle of Budweiser)
OPENING HOURS: Open hours vary but it usually shuts at 11.00pm.
FOUNDED: 1902 originally, reopened in 2003.
CAPACITY: 350
SOME ACTS WHO'VE PLAYED HERE: REM, Kings Of Leon, Lambchop, Nick Cave and the Bad Seeds, Grandaddy, Nitin Sawhney, Beth Orton, Kings of Leon, Magic Numbers, Suede, Coldplay.
WHAT'S ON? A wide mixture of classical music, jazz, folk, pop and rock with new bands showcase the 'Buzz Night' every month (check website for details).
WHAT'S THE SOUND LIKE? Good.
WHO SHOULD BANDS TALK TO ABOUT PLAYING? To play one of their 'Buzz Nights' send a demo with a brief biog to Kath Ratcliffe at the address above.
WHAT'S THE DEAL FOR BANDS? On 'Buzz Nights' the bands have to sell (ie buy) 15 tickets in advance. Otherwise bands usually split the door between them, minus £350 running costs.
HOW DO WE GET THERE? From Shepherds Bush tube (Hammersmith And City line) turn right down Uxbridge Road. Ignore the sign at the tube station giving directions to Bush Theatre – that's a different place entirely.
website: www.bushhallmusic.co.uk

Bush Hall is roughly the size and shape of north London's gritty rock dive The Garage but that's where the similarity ends; unless you can imagine a

Rock London 2006

Bush Hall

version of The Garage that looks like it's been hollowed out of a kind of Edwardian wedding cake. Which seems unlikely. The interior is ridiculously beautiful and ornate with trumpet-playing cherubs lining the walls and chandeliers dangling from the ceiling, allowing relatively small bands the kind of flatteringly luxurious setting that they'd normally only get from much bigger venues. It was built as a present by a mad Irishman (well, the official version is 'colourful') for one of his three daughters at the beginning of the twentieth century. Up until World War II it was in constant use for ballroom dancing and Irish music but during the war it became a grand soup kitchen and, presumably a lot of soup got spilled, because in the 50s and 60s it became a bingo hall, amusement arcade and rehearsal space for bands. After that it was a snooker hall called the Carlton Club for many years. Luckily the recent upturn in live music that's saved so many unused buildings in London came to the rescue, and in 2003 it was refurbished and turned into a music school for children, and a uniquely classy small venue.

CAERNARVON CASTLE
ADDRESS: 7 - 9 Chalk Farm Rd, Camden Town
PHONE: 020 7284 0219
MANAGER: Dan Griffith
DOOR PRICE: £3 - £6 (free on Sat / Sun)
PRICE OF THEIR MOST POPULAR PINT OR BOTTLE:
£2.50 (pint of Stella Artois), £2.40 (Kronenbourg), £1.80 (Carling).
OPENING HOURS: 12.00pm – 1.30am
FOUNDED: probably 19th century
CAPACITY: 150
SOME ACTS WHO'VE PLAYED HERE: The Clash had a Saturday night residency for a time in the 70s, The Others, Babyshambles.
WHAT'S ON? Club Fabulous (Mon + Thurs), Cub Fandango (Tues), Club Riot (Weds), Last Rockers Club (Fri). Covers bands (Sat / Sun).
WHAT'S THE SOUND LIKE? OK
WHO SHOULD BANDS TALK TO ABOUT PLAYING? Send demos

to Dan Griffith at the address above or get in contact with the promoters direct at the websites below.
WHAT'S THE DEAL FOR BANDS? Depends on promoter.
HOW DO WE GET THERE? Turn right out of Camden tube station on to the High Street (which immediately turns into Chalk Farm Road) and it's on the right.
website: www.clubfandango.co.uk (promoter) www.clubfabulous.co.uk (promoter)

Even its most ardent supporter would have to admit that The Caernarvon Castle is a bit of a dump but it does have a small bonus in (drum roll) the cheapest beer of any venue in this book. This is quite impressive when you consider that it's on Camden's main drag halfway in between The Electric Ballroom and The Barfly. It's an odd place with a stage that seems slightly too big for the pub dumped halfway down one wall opposite the bar. Much more than other pubs in Camden that put on bands, this one is absolutely dominated by the music, there are few places to sit, there's nowhere to go to chat if you're confronted with some terrible blues jam, and yet they don't seem to make all that much of an effort to advertise the fact that bands play there. At the time of writing the estimable Club Fandango have started a night on Tuesdays as a sort of starter gig for bands who aren't yet big enough to play the Dublin Castle round the corner so maybe that will be the start of better things to come.

CARGO
ADDRESS: 83 Rivington Street, Shoreditch, EC2A 3AY
PHONE: 020 7749 7841 (office, not tickets)
PROMOTER: Keith Montana
DOOR PRICE: From £3 to £12
PRICE OF THEIR MOST POPULAR PINT OR BOTTLE:
£3.20 (can of Red Stripe)

The Bees Live at Cargo

Opening Hours: 11.00am – 1.00am (Mon – Thurs), 11.00am – 3.00am (Fri / Sat) 11.00am – 12.00am (Sun)
Founded: 2000
Capacity: 500
Some acts who've played here: Royksopp, The Rapture, The Bees, Sage Francis, Mint Royale, Tom McRae
What's on? Tues Demo City (new bands night). Weds (funk, drum'n'bass), Thurs Giles Peterson (house DJ) Fri (house / break beats) Sat (Asian Flavas club). (Nights vary, check website for details)
What's the sound like? Very powerful and bass-y.
Who should bands talk to about playing? Send demos to Keith Montana at Arch 462 Kingsland Viaduct, 83 Rivington Street, Shoreditch EC2A
What's the deal for bands? By negotiation.
How do we get there? The nearest tube station is Old Street. Take the Hoxton Square exit then head down Old Street till you get to Great Eastern Street. Rivington Street is a very narrow, very easy to miss, street on the left. Check the website for a map and directions.
website: www.cargo-london.com

Everything from the fashionably exposed brickwork, to the swish menu and the fact that they don't sell beer on draught tells you that Cargo is far from your normal toilet venue. As with most of the bars and clubs in the area this one's hollowed out of a small chunk of Britain's industrial decay so it sits snugly under three railway arches in what was once an insalubrious little alley in the backstreets of the East End but which is now home to several cool bars and restaurants. They've divided it neatly into a bar / restaurant on one side and a trendily austere venue with another bar at the back on the other. The soundsystem is designed for bassy dance music so it does leave you feeling like you're being pinned to the wall but this is not necessarily a bad thing. Since it opened Cargo has steadily increased the emphasis on live music and, although it's still hugely popular as a club, the Demo City nights on Tuesdays are a good source of new bands that eschew the standard guitar rock formula you'll find in most small venues.

CATCH
ADDRESS: 22 Kingsland Road, Shoreditch, E2 8DA
PHONE: 020 7729 6097
PROMOTER: Chandra
DOOR PRICE: free
PRICE OF THEIR MOST POPULAR PINT OR BOTTLE:
£2.80 (bottle of Grolsch or Stella)
OPENING HOURS: 4.30pm-11.00pm (Tues / Weds) 4.30pm-2.00am (Thurs / Fri) 6pm-2.00am (Sat) 6.00pm-1.00am (Sun)
FOUNDED: 2000 as Catch (nineteenth century as a pub)
CAPACITY: 150 (+ 100 in the bar downstairs)
SOME ACTS WHO'VE PLAYED HERE: The Libertines, Ikara Colt, The Others, Towers Of London, The Beat Up, The Long Blondes
WHAT'S ON? Three bands a night on two Thursdays a month, clubbing most other nights with occasional live bands. Check website for details.
WHAT'S THE SOUND LIKE? Not terribly good.
WHO SHOULD BANDS TALK TO ABOUT PLAYING? Send demos to Chandra or get in touch with their regular promoters.
WHAT'S THE DEAL FOR BANDS? Depends on the promoter but if bands approach the venue wanting to play they ask them to organise a night themselves, booking support acts, DJs etc and they get 10% of the bar-take.
HOW DO WE GET THERE? Nearest tube is Old Street Station. Take exit 2 and turn left down Old Street past the Holiday Inn Express hotel and Kingsland Road is on your left. Catch is next door to the club Herbal on the right.
website: www.thecatchbar.com

Catch is a ridiculously impractical venue but somehow it just about works. The downstairs bit is a scruffy DJ bar with solid wooden booths and an atmosphere that borrows heavily from old man's pub chic while being thoroughly Shoreditch (ie painfully trendy) at heart. Upstairs is a small L-shaped club which apparently used to host a boxing ring in the days when Shoreditch was still a hard, working class place best known for Jack The Ripper rather than designer bars. The strange shape means that bands play on a tiny corner stage with people watching them on two sides. Even then only about a fifth of the crowd can see them properly and, what with the somewhat shonky sound, the success of the place depends very much on intangible things like 'vibe'. If you were paying to get in this might not be acceptable but considering all gigs are free it would be somewhat churlish to complain. On one occasion the band ended up passing a hat around to pay for the hire of the drum kit (they raised about 20p) so they probably don't make a fortune but the atmosphere might make up for that. Shoreditch types are supposed to be ultra-cool and hard to please but this seems to be a fallacy because, unlike in Camden say, the sheer fact of seeing a real, live band on stage seems to get the crowd hugely excited.

CLAPHAM GRAND

ADDRESS: Clapham Grand, 21-25 St John's Hill, Battersea, SW11 1TT
PHONE: 020 7223 6523
MANAGER (live music): Lynton De Silva
DOOR PRICE: £10
PRICE OF THEIR MOST POPULAR PINT OR BOTTLE:
£3 (pint of Kronenbourg)
OPENING HOURS: 9.00pm- 3:00am
FOUNDED: 1900
CAPACITY: 1500 (200 downstairs for live music nights on Wednesdays)
SOME ACTS WHO'VE PLAYED HERE: The Kinks, Mercury Rev, Gil Scott Heron, The Clash, Manic Street Preachers, The Verve, The Beautiful

South, Oasis (all many years ago).
WHAT'S ON? Bands every Wednesday, various club nights the rest of the week (check website)
WHAT'S THE SOUND LIKE? Good.
WHO SHOULD BANDS TALK TO ABOUT PLAYING? At the time of writing a new booker was just about to start. Check website for details or send demos to Lynton De Silva at the address above.
WHAT'S THE DEAL FOR BANDS? Small bands playing downstairs have to buy 50 tickets at £2 each with a view to re-selling them at £5 each. For larger bands it's negotiable.
HOW DO WE GET THERE? It's virtually opposite Clapham Junction train station (ten minutes from Victoria). Turn right out of the station.
website: www.theclaphamgrand.com

For a long time nobody seemed to know what to do with this beautiful old theatre. In the nineties it narrowly escaped being turned into one of pub chain Wetherspoons cheapo booze halls but then suffered almost as terrible a fate by being made to play host to some of the cheesiest club nights in South London. It was the kind of place that people end up at after heading down to Clapham under the illusion that it's a cool place to hang out, only to discover that it's a soulless void of trustafarians, drunk Australians and rat-faced hoodlums trying to rob them. Once upon a time, though, decent bands did play here and in the last year, after a major refit and relaunch, they've started putting new, unsigned acts on again on Wednesdays. It always seems slightly pointless for small bands to play big venues where they have to put up money in advance but I suppose if they're desperate to play somewhere 'nice' then they don't have much choice. South London and Clapham in particular needs somewhere like this and since the refit it has a similarly classiness to Koko in North London. Now all it needs are bands that can actually fill it.

COBDEN CLUB

ADDRESS: 170-172 Kensal Road, Notting Hill W10 5BN
PHONE: 020 8960 4222 (venue) 020 8830 8268 (promoter)
PROMOTER: Christian Barnes (outside promoter, 4sticks live)
DOOR PRICE: £4 (Mon / Tues)
PRICE OF THEIR MOST POPULAR PINT OR BOTTLE: £3 bottle of Lapin
OPENING HOURS: 7.30pm – 1.00am (Mon / Tues (for 4Sticks live. It's a private members club the rest of the week)
FOUNDED: 1870s
CAPACITY: 200 (in the main hall)
SOME ACTS WHO'VE PLAYED HERE: Amy Winehouse, Tom Baxter, KT Tunstall.
WHAT'S ON? On Mondays and Tuesdays 4sticks live present singer-songwriters and tasteful, not-too-noisy bands. It's guestlist only but you just need to e-mail the promoter christian@4stickslive.com to get in.
WHAT'S THE SOUND LIKE? Excellent.
WHO SHOULD BANDS TALK TO ABOUT PLAYING? Send a demo to Christian Barnes at 23 Canalot Studios, 222 Kensal Road, London, W10 5BN
WHAT'S THE DEAL FOR BANDS? If they bring 35 people or over they get £1 for each person.
HOW DO WE GET THERE? Nearest tube station is Westbourne Park less than 10 minutes walk away but it's a slightly dodgy area late at night. Members probably arrive by taxi.
website: www.4stickslive.com (promoter) www.cobdenclub.co.uk (venue)

If there's a less rock'n'roll rock venue in London than the Cobden I've certainly never been there. Named after a Tory MP known for his part in the repeal of the Corn Laws it looks like a mid-priced hotel until you get into the main hall which is lavishly, if somewhat tastelessly, decorated with huge mirrors, dark burgundy wood and those little cubes of leather that some bars seem to prefer to chairs. It has two big selling points. The first is the splendid Victorian stage at one end and the second is the amazingly velvety sound from the state-of-the-art PA. It's like being passed the music on one of those silver dishes that poncey bars (like this one) give you your change on. For this reason, and for the fact that it's in an area surrounded by major record labels, The Cobden works more as a 'showcase' for new music rather than your typical venue. It's a private members club so you can't just swagger up there, you have to be on the guest list, but it does become marginally more democratic on Mondays and Tuesdays when promoters 4Sticks Live take it over. They put on unsigned acts with the emphasis on marketable talent and technical ability rather than the shambolic passion and bludgeoning enthusiasm that you get in London's more traditional new music haunts. If that sounds like a compliment then The Cobden might be worth a visit.

THE CORONET

ADDRESS: The Coronet, 26-28 New Kent Rd, Elephant and Castle, SE1 6TJ.
PHONE: 020 7701 1500.
MANAGER: John Hobbs
DOOR PRICE: £10 - £40
PRICE OF THEIR MOST POPULAR PINT OR BOTTLE:
£3 (pint of Carling)
OPENING HOURS: It's usually open one or two nights a week. 7.00pm – (up to) 6.00am (depending on what's on).
FOUNDED: early 19th century as a theatre.
CAPACITY: 2200
SOME ACTS WHO'VE PLAYED HERE: Blur, The Beta Band, Oasis, Charlie Chaplin.
WHAT'S ON? Not much yet but big bands (like Oasis) are starting to

arrive and there are plans to put on new band nights in the future.

WHAT'S THE SOUND LIKE? When it first re-opened it was pretty poor.

WHO SHOULD BANDS TALK TO ABOUT PLAYING? Check website to see if new band nights have started.

WHAT'S THE DEAL FOR BANDS? n/a

HOW DO WE GET THERE? It's next to Elephant And Castle mainline train station. Nearest tube is Elephant And Castle on the Northern and Bakerloo lines (follow the signs to the British Rail station).

website: www.coronet-london.co.uk

Like most venues of its size in London The Coronet has served time as a cinema but it started life as a theatre in the early nineteenth century. It's best known as the place where Charlie Chaplin first stepped on stage (he was born nearby). Unfortunately, if you'd been stuck on a corner of the awesomely horrendous bit of South London that is Elephant & Castle for over a hundred years then you'd look pretty rough, too and The Coronet certainly looks its age. Inside it's like the gutted hulk of a battle ship, with columns in all the wrong places and a sound that struggles with dreadful acoustics. With its sloping floor it could be a distant cousin of the Brixton Academy a few miles down the road but only if that distant cousin had spent several years turning trick for crack. The area is in the middle of some serious regeneration and the reopening of The Coronet in 2003 was part of that. Unusually for one of London's great twentieth century cinemas they're actually putting on films again and if they could just sort out the sound and entice a few more bands down here it could become part of a new era for Elephant And Castle, which is also slowly being regenerated.

THE DUBLIN CASTLE

ADDRESS: 94 Parkway, Camden, NW1 7AN
PROMOTER: Bugbear Promotions (Jim Mattison and Tony Gleed)
DOOR PRICE: Free into the pub. Sun-Thurs: £5 (£4.50cons) Fri-Sat £6 (£4.50cons) for the bands.
PRICE OF THEIR MOST POPULAR PINT OR BOTTLE: £2.90 (pint of Becks)
OPENING HOURS: 12.00pm-midnight Sunday to Thursday. 12.00pm-1.00am Friday-Saturday.
FOUNDED: 1900s as a pub. 1960s as a music venue.
CAPACITY: 112
SOME ACTS WHO'VE PLAYED HERE: Madness, Blur, Keane, Travis, Idlewild, Tindersticks, Stereophonics.
WHAT'S ON? Bands most nights including the excellent Club Fandango on Tuesdays.
WHAT'S THE SOUND LIKE? Good.
WHO SHOULD BANDS TALK TO ABOUT PLAYING? Send a demo to Tony or Jim at Bugbear Promotions c/o The Dublin Castle (see above). Or else get in contact with Club Fandango (see website below).
WHAT'S THE DEAL FOR BANDS? New bands get 60% of the door after they've taken £75 on the Bugbear nights. Bigger bands can be offered guarantees. Check with promoters for other nights.
HOW DO WE GET THERE? From Camden Town tube station exit on to the High Street, cross over the road to Parkway and it's a couple of hundred yards down on the right.
website: www.bugbearbookings.com www.clubfandango.co.uk

While the Barfly round the corner can currently lay claim to being the spiritual home of indie in London, the Dublin Castle offers a friendlier, less up-itself take on the same. This is quite an achievement considering the scruffier fringes of the music industry (journalists, indie A&Rs etc) have made it, if not exactly a second home, at least a third or fourth. Supposedly the name of the pub comes from the nineteenth century when the railway was being built. The navvies of different nationalities kept getting into fights so the authorities allocated them a pub each: The Windsor Castle for the English, The Pembroke Castle for the Welsh, The Edinburgh Castle for the Scottish and this place for the Irish. Until recently the latter were still a big part of the place but the change in clientele is symbolised by the signed message from Madness on the back wall of the narrow front bar. Since Suggs and co played the back room it's never been the same but, despite the hordes of junk-shop-clothed indie types who've traipsed through in the last twenty five years, you never feel that the original railway workers would be turning in their grave. There's still a proper pub here, rather than just a music venue and that's a big part of its charm.

EARL'S COURT

ADDRESS: Warwick Road, SW5 9TA
PHONE 020 7385 1200 (office) 0870 903 9033 (tickets)
MANAGER: n/a
DOOR PRICE: varies depending on artist and ticket but usually from £25 - £50.
PRICE OF THEIR MOST POPULAR PINT OR BOTTLE:
£3.10 (pint of Carling)
OPENING HOURS: usually 8.00pm – 11.00pm for concerts.
FOUNDED: 1937
CAPACITY: 18500 (all seated) to 20000 (mixture of seated and standing).
SOME ACTS WHO'VE PLAYED HERE: Radiohead, Kylie Minogue, Led Zeppelin, Oasis, U2, Muse.
WHAT'S ON? Huge bands a couple of times a month.
WHAT'S THE SOUND LIKE? OK, for an arena.
WHO SHOULD BANDS TALK TO ABOUT PLAYING? n/a

WHAT'S THE DEAL FOR BANDS? n/a
HOW DO WE GET THERE? From Earl's Court tube station take the Warwick Road exit and it's right in front of you.
website: www.eco.co.uk

Until Earl's Court was built in 1937 this area was just a patch of wasteland in between criss-crossing train-tracks. If you go and see a band there now you might not notice all that much difference in the atmosphere from when the only excitement was the occasional train crash. The standing area right in front of the stage is not too bad but the banks of seats that run down either side are laughably far away with a ridiculous view. The only positive thing that you can say about the place is that there are certain kinds of bands who can come to a place like this and grab it by its horrible bucket seats and rattle it till the stuffed cash registers at the front chime like maracas. Fans still have happy memories of the time Oasis played the biggest indoor gigs in Britain here, while U2 and Muse have also relished the challenge of trying to communicate with the distant stick-figures at the back of the arena. Unfortunately, though, you can often be reminded that this place's natural inhabitant is the Ideal Home Exhibition, which turns up every year. Anywhere that provides a home to Daily Mail-reading lovers of novelty tin-openers is not an obvious place to go and see a band.

ELBOW ROOMS
ADDRESS: 89-91 Chapel Market, Islington N1
PHONE: 020 7278 3244
PROMOTER: Andy Peyton
DOOR PRICE: £5 (Thursdays) £4 (Mondays)
PRICE OF THEIR MOST POPULAR PINT: £1.50 for a bottle of Carling (special offer on Thursdays only). £3 for a pint of Grolsch.
OPENING HOURS: 12.00pm – 2.00am
FOUNDED: 2000

CAPACITY: 400 – 500 for gigs (600 normally)
SOME ACTS WHO'VE PLAYED HERE: Elbow, Ash, Soulwax, The Rapture, The Noisettes, Chikinki, The Mau Maus.
WHAT'S ON? Bands every Thursday night (currently it's 'Disturbance' for alternative urban sounds on the first of the month, Goldie Rocks for electro / indie on the second, Young And Lost for new bands on the third, Circus for bigger indie / rock acts on the fourth.) Mondays also occasionally see unsigned bands.
WHAT'S THE SOUND LIKE? Good.
WHO SHOULD BANDS TALK TO ABOUT PLAYING? Send demos to Andy Peyton at the address above.
WHAT'S THE DEAL FOR BANDS? Negotiable, depending on promoter (no deposit or pay to play).
HOW DO WE GET THERE? Nearest tube station is Angel. Cross over the road and turn right towards Liverpool Road, which is diagonally opposite the station. Chapel Market is a little way down on the left and The Elbow Room is near the other end of the street.
website: www.theelbowroom.co.uk

The Elbow Rooms are a chain of pool bars across the UK (well, London and Leeds so far) but they give each one a fair degree of independence and the Islington version is currently all about music. It's been tried before when legendary producer Arthur Baker (New Order and many others) put on an afternoon called 'Sunday Jam' with some great new bands but the PA and the stage was never quite up to it. But, from February 2005 onwards the music has been given almost as much prominence as the pool. 'Almost' is an important rider, of course, because the ambience is a little unusual. The stage is shoved in one corner while all around people are still playing pool as the band plays. This can give it the atmosphere of a gig in a Hollywood film where something much more important is going on in the foreground. As a bar, though, the Elbow Room is well worth visiting in its own right. The atmosphere is apparently based on New York pool halls with big leather booths, polished wood and lighting that makes everybody look that little bit cooler than they do in real life. This means it's not the ideal place for jumping up and down and spilling beer over yourself but as a night out it's worth taking a punt.

ELECTRIC BALLROOM

ADDRESS: The Electric Ballroom, 184 Camden High Street, NW1
PHONE: 020 7485 9006 (booking information) 020 7485 9007 (office)
MANAGER: Brian Wheeler
DOOR PRICE: from £7 - £15
PRICE OF THEIR MOST POPULAR PINT OR BOTTLE:
£3.10 (pint of Kronenbourg)
OPENING HOURS: 7.00pm – 10.30pm or 11.00pm (gig nights) 10.30pm – 3.00am or 3.30am (club nights)
FOUNDED: 1938 (as The Carousel) 1978 (as The Electric Ballroom)
CAPACITY: 1100
SOME ACTS WHO'VE PLAYED HERE: Madness, The Clash, The Smiths, Blur, Garbage, Blink 182, Oasis, U2, Red Hot Chilli Peppers, Public Enemy.
WHAT'S ON? Several relatively big name bands a month plus various club nights, currently including Sin City on Fridays (hard rock, metal, hip-hop), Shake on Saturdays (disco, R&B, 70s). Plus they often host record fairs during the day. Check website for details.
WHAT'S THE SOUND LIKE? OK
WHO SHOULD BANDS TALK TO ABOUT PLAYING? All gigs are put on by outside promoters, don't send demos to management.
WHAT'S THE DEAL FOR BANDS? Depends on promoter
HOW DO WE GET THERE? Turn right out of Camden tube station on to the high street and it's about twenty metres on your right.
website: www.electric-ballroom.co.uk

In the 40s the bit of Camden High Street where the Electric Ballroom stands had the misfortune to be next door to a munitions factory. This meant that when it was bombed in WWII an entire terrace of houses was destroyed, killing 12 people. This puts the venue's current travails into perspective. Their only misfortune is to find themselves on a bit of real estate that London Underground are eyeing up. The Tube Station desperately needs to be expanded (as anyone who has squeezed through it at the weekend with thousands of pierced goths will know) and London Underground want to fund the expansion by knocking down the same stretch of street that was destroyed by the Luftwaffe 50 years ago: this time to build a shopping mall and luxury apartments. For the time being the Electric Ballroom seems to be safe, a June 2005 enquiry turned London Underground's plans down, but they're still waiting to see what happens next. The long legal battle has already cost the owners around £2 million pounds and the drain on resources has almost became a slow death in itself. At the moment the venue's surviving on its atmosphere and reputation but it's in serious need of refurbishment. Ironically the only reason that anyone wants to build a shopping mall in Camden is to leech off the thousands of tourists who come from all over the world to sample the unique atmosphere that places like the Electric Ballroom represent.

THE END

ADDRESS: 18 West Central Street, WC1A 1JJ
PHONE: 0207 419 9199
PROMOTER: Erol Alkan (for Trash, on Mondays only)
DOOR PRICE: £5 to £15 (£6 for Trash, discounts sometimes available from the website).
PRICE OF THEIR MOST POPULAR PINT OR BOTTLE:
£3.50 (pint of Kronenbourg)
OPENING HOURS: 10.00pm – 3.00am
FOUNDED: 1995
CAPACITY: 1000

SOME ACTS WHO'VE PLAYED HERE: Fatboy Slim, Daft Punk, Zero 7, Death From Above 1979, Laurent Garnier, Roni Size, Peaches, Yeah Yeah Yeahs, LCD Sound System, The Rapture, Erase Errata, Kaito, Relaxed Muscle, Zoot Woman, Wolfman.

WHAT'S ON? Various clubs six nights a week including electro / rock night Trash on Mondays, plus drum and bass, breaks, house and techno on other nights (check website for details). Guitar-based bands tend to play Trash on Mondays but top DJs and dance acts also make regular appearances on other nights.

WHAT'S THE SOUND LIKE? Excellent.

WHO SHOULD BANDS TALK TO ABOUT PLAYING? Interested bands should contact info@endclub.com and they'll forward requests but don't hold your breath.

WHAT'S THE DEAL FOR BANDS? Negotiable (no deposit or pay to play).

HOW DO WE GET THERE? It's a five-minute walk from Holborn and Tottenham Court Road tube stations or there are numerous night buses from Tottenham Court Road (check website for map).

website: www.endclub.com

Many well-meaning government types, parents, teachers, doctors and psychiatrists have tried to convince kids that taking drugs isn't cool but none have been so successful as The End's co-founder Mr C. As a rapper for 90s dance act The Shamen his attempt to pin down dance culture in a novelty song with 'Ebeneezer Goode' and it's famous "E's are good" chorus reduced ecstasy to the status of a Bacardi Breezer and started dance culture's long decline. Well, that's one theory. But then The End also showed the way forward for the clubs that were left stranded by the credibility gap that came in his gibbering wake. They started by getting details like the sound and acoustics right but they also led the way in expanding beyond the tired Super-DJ formula. Mondays' long running Trash club was greeted with ravenous approval by kids who loved indie music but who regarded themselves as far too cool and sexy to go to the traditional sticky-floored indie disco. It's been running for too long to have quite the same cachet now but they still put on good bands, crammed along a narrow wall on a low stage while an eager, mostly student crowd try to dance in the crammed space in front. For the bands, with the metallic walls and gleaming surfaces, it must be like playing inside a space-aged biscuit tin but then again if the biscuits are right the tin doesn't really matter.

THE ENTERPRISE

ADDRESS: 2 Haverstock Hill, NW3
PHONE: 020 7485 2659
PROMOTER: The Barfly promoters (Jeremy Ledlin and Michael Nicholas)
DOOR PRICE: £5
PRICE OF THEIR MOST POPULAR PINT OR BOTTLE: £2.90 (pint of Grolsch)
OPENING HOURS: bands usually on 7.00pm – 11.00pm
FOUNDED: 2003 as a music venue.
CAPACITY: 50
SOME ACTS WHO'VE PLAYED HERE: Queens Of The Stone Age, Ian Broudie, The Crimea.
WHAT'S ON? Acoustic bands / singer-songwriters / etc.
WHAT'S THE SOUND LIKE? Good.
WHO SHOULD BANDS TALK TO ABOUT PLAYING? Send demos to Barfly Bookings, 59-61 Farringdon Road, London, EC1M 3JB
WHAT'S THE DEAL FOR BANDS? For small bands the first ten people they bring cover the costs and after that they get a percentage of the door. For larger bands it's negotiable.
HOW DO WE GET THERE? Nearest tube station is Chalk Farm. Turn right out of the station and it's diagonally opposite.
website: www.barfly.com

It would be easy to describe The Enterprise as The Barfly's little brother but as soon as you step through the door you'll realise that's not quite right. The Barfly is just down the road and they host a tiny 'Barfly Acoustic' night upstairs here but downstairs the feeling is at least older brother if not great-grandfather to the brasher Camden venue. It's Irish in a posh, literary way with packed bookcases and pictures of WB Yeats and George Bernard Shaw around the walls, as well as a statue of Oscar Wilde above the door. This might make it sound like some kind of theme bar but it doesn't come across like that. Despite being almost opposite Chalk Farm Road tube it's far enough away from the Camden throng to have preserved a friendly, local atmosphere. Upstairs where bands play the atmosphere is endearingly amateurish with manky chairs and tables set up in front of a low stage. It's a very Camden version of the kind of sophisticated, adult easy-listening set up that you get elsewhere and that's a good thing. They used to have punk gigs here in the 70s but the new, more laidback set-up suits it perfectly.

FABRIC

ADDRESS: 77a Charterhouse St, Farringdon EC1M 3HN
PHONE: 020 7336 8898
GENERAL MANAGER: Dan Coshan
DOOR PRICE: £10 - £15
PRICE OF THEIR MOST POPULAR PINT OR BOTTLE:
£3.50 for a bottle of Stella Artois.
OPENING HOURS: usually 9.30pm – 5.00am (Fridays) 10.00pm – 7.00am (Sat). Very occasionally open on weekdays but usually just for private parties etc (check website for details).
FOUNDED: 1999
CAPACITY: 1600
SOME ACTS WHO'VE PLAYED HERE: Scissor Sisters, Soulwax, Death In Vegas, Nitin Sawney, Ian Brown, Aim, Talvin Singh, Isaac Hayes! Two Lone Swordsman, Dizzy Rascal, The Freestylers, Hybrid, Mylo,

Royksopp.
WHAT'S ON? Fabric Live (Fridays) for live music from big name electronic / crossover acts. Fabric (Saturdays) for house, techno, breaks and occasional live acts.
WHAT'S THE SOUND LIKE? Excellent.
WHO SHOULD BANDS TALK TO ABOUT PLAYING? Steve Blonde or Shaun Roberts (book Fabric live on Fridays), Judy Griffith.
WHAT'S THE DEAL FOR BANDS? Negotiable.
HOW DO WE GET THERE? Getting there should be easy as it's not far from Farringdon (just round the corner) Barbican and Chancery Lane tube stations. Getting home might be harder as there are few buses and even fewer night buses in this area. Get a cab if you can afford it, the club operate their own taxi firm.
website: www.fabriclondon.com

A lot of people date the death of club culture in Britain to New Year's Eve 1999. Maybe the drugs were starting to wear off but paying £100 to listen to a bloke spinning records suddenly started to seem a bit silly. This should have been bad news for Fabric which had opened earlier that year but instead they established themselves as the one 'superclub' that didn't suddenly seem as tacky and tawdry as a FCUK t-shirt. This was just as well as it must have cost the owners a fortune to fit the place out with the incredible soundsystem (since updated several times) and fancy lighting. Encouragingly for those who still prefer their entertainment to come from people doing a little more than "pointing to someone in the crowd and smiling" ("super DJ" Paul Oakenfold's explanation for what he did to earn his enormous wodge of cash) they've also started putting on live music. The Scissor Sisters played one of their first British gigs here and all kinds of dance-y, electronic types have played at Fabric Live on Fridays or on other club nights. It's become routine to hear Fabric described as London or Britain's best club and that has almost become a millstone as the place is in danger of becoming the kind of 'event' venue

frequented by confused hen nights but, with a bit of a luck, the cavernous meat cellar halls, cool Clerkenwell location and distinct lack of cheese will keep Fabric firmly in the underground.

FIDDLER'S ELBOW: Come Down And Meet The Folks.
ADDRESS: 1 Malden Road, NW5 3HS
PHONE: 020 7485 3269
PROMOTER: Alan Tyler (Sundays)
DOOR PRICE: free
PRICE OF THEIR MOST POPULAR PINT OR BOTTLE:
£2.50 (pint of Fosters)
OPENING HOURS: 4.00pm – 8.00pm Sundays (Come Down And Meet The Folks)
FOUNDED: unknown. Come Down And Meet The Folks has been here since 2003
CAPACITY: 150 (approx)
SOME ACTS WHO'VE PLAYED HERE: The Broken Family Band, Boz Boorer, The Izzys.

WHAT'S ON? 'Come Down And Meet The Folks' on Sunday afternoons for blues, folk and bluegrass. Occasional live music on other nights.
WHAT'S THE SOUND LIKE? Fine
WHO SHOULD BANDS TALK TO ABOUT PLAYING? To play Sundays turn up at 5.00pm and talk to Alan Tyler or contact him via the website below.
WHAT'S THE DEAL FOR BANDS? Small guarantee plus a hat is passed around.
HOW DO WE GET THERE? Nearest tube is Chalk Farm. Turn left out of the station and take Prince Of Wales road, which is a little way down on the right. The pub is on the corner of Malden Road.
website: www.comedownandmeetthefolks.co.uk

Maybe it was the name but I was expecting this place to be full of bearded types in chunky woollen sweaters enjoying earnest tunes about crops failing. Instead, on a Sunday afternoon when 'Come Down And Meet The Folks' come to visit it's heaving with one of the oddest crowds you'll see at a gig anywhere in London. It's as though every era of pop culture in the last forty years has sent a representative, so there are authentic teddy boys with greased back quiffs and drape jackets, hippies with hair down their shoulders and unkempt beards, women in long dresses swaying drunkenly to distorted rockabilly, portly blokes peering through cracked glasses and, most disturbingly, one small boy in a kind of sci-fi Roman Emperor costume attacking people with a kind of toy alligator. Although possibly he's not there every week. What makes it even stranger is that the pub, with it's nice, pot-plant studded décor, looks like the sort of place you'd take your gran for Sunday lunch. Frankly I found it disturbing and scary but everybody else seemed to be having a better time than they'd any right to on a rainy Sunday afternoon. Most of the time the vibe is less rockabilly and more folky but it's good to know that pockets of eccentricity like this can still survive.

FILTHY MACNASTY'S WHISKEY BAR

ADDRESS: 68 Amwell Street, Clerkenwell, EC1
PHONE: 020 7837 6067
OWNER: Paul
DOOR PRICE: usually free.
PRICE OF THEIR MOST POPULAR PINT OR BOTTLE:
£2.80 (pint of Guinness)
OPENING HOURS: 12.00pm – 11.00pm
FOUNDED: 1980s as Filthy McNasty's (nineteenth century as The Fountain pub)
CAPACITY: 80 (in the backroom) 120 in total
SOME ACTS WHO'VE PLAYED HERE: Pete And Carl from The Libertines, Hope Of The States, Beth Orton, Alabama 3, Primal Scream (DJing).
WHAT'S ON? Regular nights include Reggae Shack (DJs first Saturday of the month); Islington Blues Club (with bands and DJs first Friday of the month); literary readings night The Sharper Word (usually on a Wednesday). Check website for details.
WHAT'S THE SOUND LIKE? OK
WHO SHOULD BANDS TALK TO ABOUT PLAYING? Send demos to Veronique Morato at the address above (bearing in mind that their licence means they can only put on soloists or duos).
WHAT'S THE DEAL FOR BANDS? By negotiation but as gigs tend to be free it won't be much.
HOW DO WE GET THERE? Nearest tube station is Angel. Turn left out of the station and then take the first right down Pentonville Road then the second left down Claremont Close, which pretty quickly turns into Amwell Street. King's Cross tube is also nearby.
website: www.filthymacnastys.com

The current owner of Filthy MacNasty's spent an hour or so cleaning graffiti off the walls of the flats upstairs when he first took the bar over. He regrets it now as he could've charged obsessive Libertines fans a fortune to see the early daubings of Pete and Carl who both lived, worked as barmen and scrawled existential poetry on the walls here in the late 90s. Filthy's started life as a pub called The Fountain mainly frequented by patrons of the betting shop opposite but in the 80s sometime Pogues manager Gerry O'Boyle (who now runs the equally ace Boogaloo bar in Highgate) decided to take it over and turn it into the rock'n'roll pub of his fevered dreams. It worked almost too well. Shane McGowan rarely left his spot by the bar, Johnny Depp dropped in all the time when he was filming 'From Hell' and it became known as the kind of place where anything could happen. Unfortunately 'anything' tends not to mean a few quiet pints and a nice game of billiards. After complaints from the locals about noise and rowdiness the pub had its licence revoked and it was shut for about six months. Since then it's been re-opened and tarted up a bit with the usual leather sofas in the saloon bar and a new line up of literary nights, music etc in the tiny back room. Pete and Carl obviously still like it, though. At the time of writing it's one of the last places they played together, back in spring 2004.

THE FORUM
ADDRESS: 9-17 Highgate Road, NW5
PHONE: 020 7284 1001
MANAGER: Ivor Wilkins / Craig Prentice
DOOR PRICE: from £8 - £35 (usually around £15)
PRICE OF THEIR MOST POPULAR PINT: £3.10 (pint of Fosters), £3.20 (can of Red Stripe)
OPENING HOURS: usually 7.00pm – 11.00pm
FOUNDED: 1934 (as a cinema), 1980s as The Town And Country Club, 1992 as The Forum.
CAPACITY: 2110 (including 760 seated)
SOME ACTS WHO'VE PLAYED HERE: The Who, Ian Dury, Robbie

Williams, Oasis, Run DMC, Wu-Tang Clan, Scissor Sisters, The Libertines, Isaac Hayes.

WHAT'S ON? Big name acts several times a month, with more hip-hop than most other venues of this size.

WHAT'S THE SOUND LIKE? Excellent.

WHO SHOULD BANDS TALK TO ABOUT PLAYING? n/a (all done through promoters).

WHAT'S THE DEAL FOR BANDS? n/a

HOW DO WE GET THERE? Nearest tube station is Kentish Town. Turn right out of the station and where the road branches off, go left past The Bull And Gate down Highgate Road and you'll see it on the left. website: www.meanfiddler.com

The Forum, like most medium sized London venues, was originally built as a cinema in the thirties. In this case they tried to make it look vaguely Roman with proper pillars and everything and, if you go there now, the layers of incredibly black grime that cover everything make it look older than most genuine Roman ruins. Many London gig goers have happy memories of the place when it was called The Town And Country Club and played host to all the best bands of the 80s but even today it's still a great place to come although, for some reason, they don't seem to have as many great bands as they used to. The acoustics are good, it doesn't take hours to get served at the bars, and even in the seated area upstairs it still feels vaguely rock'n'roll. Music fans are often accused of being elitist when they complain about their favourite band selling out but what they mean is that they wished they were still playing at a venue like this rather than a soulless megadrome. If only the bar prices weren't so ludicrously high it would be perfect.

THE GARAGE

ADDRESS: 20-22 Highbury Corner, N5 1RD
PHONE: 020 7607 1818
MANAGER: James Gall
DOOR PRICE: from £4 - £15
PRICE OF THEIR MOST POPULAR PINT OR BOTTLE: £3.10 (pint of Kronenbourg)
OPENING HOURS: usually 7.00pm – 11.00pm (clubs 11.00pm – 3.00am at the weekend).
FOUNDED: 1993
CAPACITY: 500 (downstairs) 250 (approx, upstairs)
SOME ACTS WHO'VE PLAYED HERE: Spiritualized, Catatonia, Supergrass, Placebo, Afghan Whigs, Dinosaur Jr, the Boo Radleys, Elastica, Radiohead.
WHAT'S ON? Bands most nights plus late clubs at the weekend. Don't Stop Me Now (best of 70s-00s retro 11.00pm – 3.00am Fri), International Hi-Fi (indie / classics 11.00pm-3.00am Sat). Steve Lamacq's Punk Karaoke (alternate Sats – Upstairs At The Garage).
WHAT'S THE SOUND LIKE? Excellent.
WHO SHOULD BANDS TALK TO ABOUT PLAYING? Send demos to Carina Jirsch, Mean Fiddler Music Group, 16 High Street, Harlesden, NW10 4LX (check website for guidelines)
WHAT'S THE DEAL FOR BANDS? Downstairs they usually get £1.50 for each punter who brings a flyer, as long as they bring at least 40 people. Upstairs it's the same as long as they bring at least 30.
HOW DO WE GET THERE? It's virtually opposite Highbury and Islington tube. Walk to the end of the short road leading up to the tube, turn left and it's right in front of you.
website: www.meanfiddler.com

For Americans or other out-of-towners the first thing to know about

The Garage is that it's pronounced to rhyme with marriage – probably a short, boozy and abusive one. Despite being founded by the powerful Mean Fiddler Group The Garage has an unpretentious and uncorporate atmosphere, which is almost the exact reverse of the swanky Islington Academy down the other end of the trendy-restaurant-studded Upper Street. Essentially it's just a grimy box with a stage at one end and a bar at the other. There are tables and chairs near the bar but even the most loud-mouthed A&R man won't be able to make themselves heard over the magnificently powerful sound system. It's not as if it's the sort of place where you'll feel the need to sit down and have a chat. On at least one occasion (watching the brutally loud and abrasive Alec Empire) being in The Garage has felt like being stuck inside a plane's black box recorder during a crash but that's because this is a proper place to hear bands and not just casually watch them. Until recently there was nowhere to escape although a few years ago they did open The Minibar next door and there is another slightly less atmospheric venue, Upstairs At The Garage, for smaller bands. When it's half empty there's something slightly desolate about the place but when it's full there are few livelier venues in London.

HALFMOON, PUTNEY

ADDRESS: 93 Lower Richmond Rd, SW15
PHONE: 020 8780 9383
PROMOTER: Carrie Davies
DOOR PRICE: £2.50 - £20
PRICE OF THEIR MOST POPULAR PINT OR BOTTLE:
£3 (pint of Fosters)
OPENING HOURS: usually 7.00pm – 11.00pm (in the venue)
FOUNDED: 1963 as a major music venue, although there'd been music here before that.
CAPACITY: 200
SOME ACTS WHO'VE PLAYED HERE: U2 had a residency in 1980

and played their first sell-out gig here, Rolling Stones, Kasabian, Natasha Bedingfield, Ralph McTell, The Yardbirds, Elvis Costello, Kate Bush, Rooster.

WHAT'S ON? Live music virtually every night of the week.

WHAT'S THE SOUND LIKE? Good.

WHO SHOULD BANDS TALK TO ABOUT PLAYING? Send demos to Carrie Davies at the address above (check website for guidelines).

WHAT'S THE DEAL FOR BANDS? They need to bring about 50 people (deal negotiable depending on how established the band is).

HOW DO WE GET THERE? Nearest tube is Putney Bridge on the District Line. From the station follow the sign to Putney Bridge, cross the bridge and take the first right on to Lower Richmond Road on the other side.

website: www.halfmoon.co.uk

Halfmoon, Putney

After a long period of contraction the gig circuit seems to have expanded again recently. From being focused mostly in Camden, Islington and a few places in the West End a whole host of new venues have sprung up in East London and there's been a mini-resurgence in Brixton. None of this has helped the poor, benighted folks who live in this bit of West London, though. It always seems a long way from the rest of town even though it's a lot easier to get to than, say, New Cross. This might have posed a few problems for the Halfmoon, which is an elegant Victorian pub, stuck out in the pine-floor, All Bar One land of Putney. They put on live music most nights of the week in an atmosphere which is a little less precious, pretentious and cool than other, similar sized, venues elsewhere. This means that the flavour-of-the-month plays second fiddle to the more accomplished musos who've sometimes built up a following here for years. It sounds pretty dull and it probably is if you're looking for the next big thing but then again it would be a shame if every venue in London was trying to be a clone of the Barfly.

HAMMERSMITH APOLLO

(Carling Apollo Hammersmith)
ADDRESS: Queen Caroline Street, W6 9QH
PHONE: 020 8563 3800 (office) 0870 606 3400 (tickets)
MANAGER: Phil Rogers
DOOR PRICE: £10 - £80
PRICE OF THEIR MOST POPULAR PINT OR BOTTLE:
£3.50 (pint of Grolsch)
OPENING HOURS: usually 7.30pm – 11.00pm
FOUNDED: 1932
CAPACITY: 5035 (standing) 3628 (seated)
SOME ACTS WHO'VE PLAYED HERE: David Bowie (Ziggy Stardust's last gig), Manic Street Preachers, PJ Harvey, Beck, Avril Lavigne, Public Enemy (as featured on the live intro to "It Takes A Nation Of Millions To Hold Us Back").

Rock London 2006

WHAT'S ON? Big name bands several nights a week plus comedy etc.
WHAT'S THE SOUND LIKE? Excellent.
WHO SHOULD BANDS TALK TO ABOUT PLAYING? All arranged through outside promoters.
WHAT'S THE DEAL FOR BANDS? n/a
HOW DO WE GET THERE? Hammersmith is the nearest tube on the District, Piccadilly and Hammersmith & City lines. From the Hammersmith & City line exit the venue is in front of you on the other side of the flyover. From the District & Piccadilly line exit follow the signs through the Broadway shopping centre and under the flyover.
website: www.carlinglive.com

Carling Apollo Hammersmith, as it's slightly depressingly known, used to be called the Hammersmith Odeon and older, conservative gig-goers (the type of people who regard the metric system as a sin against God) still refer to it as that. To give the old codgers their due, though, there is something almost deliberately sinister about the bronze plaque on the wall warning that it's owned by Clear Channel. Just because they own pretty much everything now doesn't mean they have to brag about it. In fact the place started life as the 'Gaumont Palace Supercinema' in 1932 and, because it's a listed building, it's still got the original sophisticated Art Deco light fittings and plasterwork. After closing for a while around the turn of the century it reopened in 2003 with its capacity increased to 5000 for a gig by AC/DC that people still talk about. Those who mourn the old Odeon should remember that The Clash, among others, always loathed the place because it was fully seated with over-officious security on hand to crush any attempt at dancing. These days they take the seats out downstairs for rock gigs and, because the floor slopes even more than the Brixton Academy's, it's easy for almost everyone to get a clear view proving that, whatever some people might say, not quite everything is getting worse.

HAMMERSMITH PALAIS

ADDRESS: 230 Shepherd Bush Road, W6 7NL
PHONE: 020 7341 5300
MANAGER (LIVE MUSIC): Dave Gaydon (head of music and promotions)
DOOR PRICE: £10 - £20 depending on the band.
PRICE OF THEIR MOST POPULAR PINT OR BOTTLE:
£3 (bottle of Budweiser)
OPENING HOURS: usually about 7.00pm, clubs go on till 3.00am.
FOUNDED: 1919
CAPACITY: 2230
SOME ACTS WHO'VE PLAYED HERE: The Smiths, The Clash, New Order, The Charlatans, Graham Coxon.
WHAT'S ON? At the time of writing there's about one band a month. Friday nights currently have the 'Classic' club for retro rave; Saturday nights is Britain's biggest club 'School Disco' for 80s/90s cheese nostalgia and mandatory school uniform dress code. There's usually a student night on Wednesdays or Thursdays. Check website for details of when bands are playing.
WHAT'S THE SOUND LIKE? OK
WHO SHOULD BANDS TALK TO ABOUT PLAYING? n/a (all done through promoters)
WHAT'S THE DEAL FOR BANDS? n/a
HOW DO WE GET THERE? Hammersmith is the nearest tube on the District, Piccadilly and Hammersmith & City lines. From the Hammersmith & City line exit turn right out of the station and then immediately left down Shepherd's Bush Road and it's a short way down on your left. From the District & Piccadilly line Shepherd's Bush Road is signposted through the Broadway Shopping Centre.
website: www.ponana.com

The Hammersmith Palais has the rare honour of having been lauded in two great songs. Joe Strummer famously sang about being harassed at a reggae night in 'White Man (In Hammersmith Palais') and Ian Dury lists it as one of his 'Reasons To Be Cheerful'. In recent years the main reason to be cheerful for a lot of punters has been the hordes of prematurely nostalgic girls in plaid miniskirts who turn up for the embarrassing 'School Disco' club on Saturdays. The venue insist things are changing this year as they try to increase the number of bands who play from one a month to one a week. The sound might not be as good as The Apollo down the road but they've taken out all the unsuitable furnishings from when it was briefly christened Hammersmith Po-Na-Na a few years ago and replaced them with a look which is, apparently, more similar to its classic heyday. Right in front of the stage the atmosphere is pretty good but the room is a strange, oblong shape so if you're at one end or another, or up on one of the balconies, you tend to feel a long way from where the action is. When the original Hammersmith Palais closed down they gave the sign on the front to Joe Strummer and for a while it seemed like the place's soul went with it. It's not back yet but maybe one day.

HOPE AND ANCHOR

ADDRESS: 207 Upper St, Islington, N1
PROMOTER: Bugbear Promotions (Jim Mattison and Tony Gleed)
DOOR PRICE: Free into the pub. Sun-Thurs: £5 (£4.50cons) Fri-Sat £6 (£4.50cons) for the bands.
PRICE OF THEIR MOST POPULAR PINT OR BOTTLE:
£2.90 (pint of Stella Artois)
OPENING HOURS: 12.00pm-midnight Sunday to Thursday. 12.00pm-1.00am Friday-Saturday.
FOUNDED: 1930s as a pub. 1970s as a music venue.
CAPACITY: 84
SOME ACTS WHO'VE PLAYED HERE: The Stranglers, The Sex

Pistols, The Cure, The Clash, The Damned, Joy Division, U2, Dexy's Midnight Runners, Ash, Madness

WHAT'S ON? "Anything with a guitar and an attitude"

WHAT'S THE SOUND LIKE? OK

WHO SHOULD BANDS TALK TO ABOUT PLAYING? Send a demo to Tony or Jim at Bugbear Promotions c/o The Dublin Castle (check website for guidelines).

WHAT'S THE DEAL FOR BANDS? New bands get 60% of the door after they've taken £75 (on the nights put on by Bugbear). Bigger bands can be offered guarantees. Check with promoters for other nights.

HOW DO WE GET THERE? Nearest tube station is Highbury and Islington on the Victoria line. Turn right out of the station and it's a couple of hundred yards down Upper Street on the right.

website: www.bugbearbookings.com

Once upon a time most of the legends of punk played at The Hope And Anchor, which is pretty incredible considering the capacity of 84, but then perhaps they just had a more laidback attitude to little things like fire regulations then. In 1984 the basement was shut by Health And Safety and it was squatted by punks, providing a haven for the hardcore scene of the time. Since then, it's never quite recovered the cache it once had. As a musical equivalent of a training bra it's not bad, though. The pub upstairs is alright if not exactly characterful but the descent into the cramped venue downstairs could, if you were feeling imaginative and optimistic, suggest that this is not just a basement but that vaguest of concepts 'the underground'. That might be some consolation to new bands who have to lug their equipment down the narrow stairs and past the packing cases. There hasn't been anything approaching a buzz around the Hope And Anchor in years but everybody's got to start somewhere.

ICA

(Institute Of Contemporary Arts)
ADDRESS: The Mall, SW1 5AH
PHONE: 020 7930 3647
MUSIC PROGRAMMER: Alan English
DOOR PRICE: £6 (£4 for members)
PRICE OF THEIR MOST POPULAR PINT OR BOTTLE:
£3 pint of Budvar
OPENING HOURS: midday - 10.30pm (Mon); midday - 1.00am (Tues – Sat); midday – 11.00pm (Sun).
FOUNDED: 1947
CAPACITY: 330
SOME ACTS WHO'VE PLAYED HERE: The Clash, Beta Band, Franz Ferdinand, Beastie Boys, Keane, Suede
WHAT'S ON? Vaguely arty but usually fairly mainstream indie pop & rock.
WHAT'S THE SOUND LIKE? Excellent.
WHO SHOULD BANDS TALK TO ABOUT PLAYING? You could try sending your demo to the music programmer (check website for up-to-date details) but they very rarely put on unsigned bands.
WHAT'S THE DEAL FOR BANDS? Negotiable.
HOW DO WE GET THERE? Nearest tube is Charing Cross. Take The Strand exit and turn right on to The Mall. The ICA is down on the right.
website: www.ica.org.uk

The ICA only do live music as a kind of after-thought to all their other activities promoting various kinds of new theatre, cinema and art but, for all that, their venue has better facilities than most. For a start there's no bar in the music bit so all the people who want to chat at the bar during your favourite band's quietest song will be elsewhere. When you're in the big black hole that serves as their theatre you can easily get absorbed in the music (as long as you can ignore the many arty punters' disconcerting urge to sit cross-legged on the sticky floor) and then you can go out into the bar / gallery area where things are suddenly much more civilised. When it's packed the bar can be very slow but the ICA is still the rare music venue that you'd actually consider coming to even if there wasn't any live music on. There's a nice café alongside and if you get here early unlike most venues there are things to do other than just get horribly drunk - various art exhibitions etc. Although there's nothing to stop you looking at the art and getting horribly drunk, if that's your thing, of course.

Full house at the ICA

ISLINGTON ACADEMY / BAR ACADEMY
(Carling Academy Islington)
ADDRESS: Carling Academy Islington, N1 Centre, 16 Parkfield Street N1 0PS
PHONE: 020 7288 4400 (venue) 0870 771 2000 (tickets)
MANAGER: Lucinda Brown
DOOR PRICE: from £3 to £20 but usually round £10

PRICE OF THEIR MOST POPULAR PINT: £2.95 (can, bottle or pint of Carling)
OPENING HOURS: bands usually 7.00pm – 11.00pm. Clubs afterwards till 2.00am in the week (when on, check listings) till 4.00am at weekends.
FOUNDED: 2002 as The Marquee, 2003 as The Islington Academy.
CAPACITY: 800 (Islington Academy) 250 (Bar Academy)
SOME ACTS WHO'VE PLAYED HERE: Bloc Party, Kasabian, Kid Carpet (Bar Academy). Muse, Craig David, The Cooper Temple Clause, Athlete, Lostprophets. The Cure. (Islington Academy).
WHAT'S ON? Bands several times a week in both venues plus Club Seal (indie) on Fridays and Ministry of Funk on Saturdays in Bar Academy.
WHAT'S THE SOUND LIKE? Excellent.
WHO SHOULD BANDS TALK TO ABOUT PLAYING? New bands interested in support slots should send a demo to Academy Events at the address above.
WHAT'S THE DEAL FOR BANDS? negotiable.
HOW DO WE GET THERE? Nearest tube station is Angel, on the Northern Line. The N1 Centre is diagonally opposite. Turn right out of the station and head about 20 yards down Upper Street and you'll see the entrance. The venue is near the back.
website: www.islington-academy.co.uk/

When it opened, this venue was supposed to be a reincarnation of the late lamented Marquee, a club that hosted many of the biggest names of the '70s. Unfortunately, that name seems to have a curse on it (a new Marquee has opened in Leicester Square so maybe that'll do better). Not long after opening it closed but it's since been rescued and rebranded by the people who run Brixton Academy. Their first problem was that to get to the venue you have to walk through a gleaming shopping centre that exudes the same louche, rock'n'roll spirit as a brand new Ford Focus. With the place also suffering from the 'Carling' prefix it'll be no surprise that this place is routinely sneered at for being 'soulless'. There's some truth in that but at least the owners have spent the sponsorship money on what, they claim, is one of the best PAs for a venue of this size in London. They could do with hiring a few more bar staff, too, as it's not hard to spend twenty minutes ordering a drink on busy nights. But, although the downstairs Academy is a little too shiny for its own good, the Bar Academy upstairs is much better than it's given credit for. There's nothing inherently wrong with venues cleaning the floor occasionally and people who claim that it's too clean are missing the point. Soul should be supplied by the people on stage, rather than by the stains in the toilets.

JAZZ CAFE

ADDRESS: 5 Parkway, Camden Town, NW1 7PG
PHONE: 020 7916 6060
MANAGER: Lisa Auger
DOOR PRICE: usually from £7 - £25
PRICE OF THEIR MOST POPULAR PINT OR BOTTLE: £3.30 (pint of Grolsch)
OPENING HOURS: 7.00pm – 1.00am (Mon / Thurs); 7.00pm – 2.00am (Fri / Sat); Jam Session midday – 4.00pm (Sun) then 7.00pm – midnight.
FOUNDED: 1990
CAPACITY: 344
SOME ACTS WHO'VE PLAYED HERE: Gil Scott Heron, James Taylor Quartet, Bert Jansch, Jungle Brothers, Kosheen, Slick Rick
WHAT'S ON? Bands / musicians most nights plus DJs.
WHAT'S THE SOUND LIKE? Good.
WHO SHOULD BANDS TALK TO ABOUT PLAYING? Contact Andy Robbins at the address above.
WHAT'S THE DEAL FOR BANDS? Negotiable
HOW DO WE GET THERE? Nearest tube is Camden. Take the exit on to the High Street, cross over the road to Parkway and it's a couple of hundred yards down on the right.

website: www.meanfiddler.com

The people who invented jazz and then turned it into the world's most demented form of music would be surprised to see it in its usual live incarnation as beardy mood music for Sunday afternoon pubs. At the Jazz Café, though, the pioneers might feel a bit more at home. Theirs is a resolutely non-purist take on the genre but jazz was never supposed to be pure anyway and, as a result, The Jazz Cafe has become the number one club in London for all kinds of genres that don't fit in more traditional pub venues. This means that, while you might get the odd band that could loosely be described as 'rock', more often they provide a space for all of jazz's cousins: soul, funk, hip-hop, house and R&B. And, unlike rock and indie fans, the patrons of this kind of music haven't yet gone for the idea that it's normal to enjoy music in venues that provide a interesting ambiguity between where the urinal ends and the rest of the venue begins. The Jazz Café used to be a bank and it's still a smart, slick sort of place with a restaurant upstairs, tables and sofas downstairs. If it was in the West End this would probably mean it would be filled with suits but in grimy Camden it's nicely out of sync with its surroundings.

KOKO

ADDRESS: 1a Camden High St, Camden, NW1 7JE
PHONE: 0870 432 5527 (tickets)
BOOKER: Daveid
DOOR PRICE: £7 for club NME (£5 with flyer). £13 for Koko Saturdays (£12 with flyer). Other nights vary.
PRICE OF THEIR MOST POPULAR PINT OR BOTTLE:
£2.60 (can of Foster's Export).
OPENING HOURS: varies. Usually bands 7.00pm – 10.00pm (when there's a club afterwards). Clubs at the weekend 10.00pm-3.00am.
FOUNDED: 2004 as Koko, 1890s as The Palace Theatre.
CAPACITY: 1410 (for gigs) 1500 (for the club)

Rock London 2006

Jump! Koko in full flow

SOME ACTS WHO'VE PLAYED HERE: The Bravery, The Concretes (as Koko). Charlie Chaplin, Sex Pistols, The Clash, Madonna, Eurythmics and thousands of others before it became Koko.

WHAT'S ON? Club NME on Fridays (indie club / bands etc), Koko Saturday on, um, Saturdays (DJs / dance music). Check website for other nights.

WHAT'S THE SOUND LIKE? Good.

WHO SHOULD BANDS TALK TO ABOUT PLAYING? Daveid@koko.uk.com (booker)

WHAT'S THE DEAL FOR BANDS? Depends on night, promoter, etc

HOW DO WE GET THERE? It's right opposite Mornington Crescent Tube station or a five minute walk from Camden Tube Station (turn left on to Camden High Street.)

website: www.koko.uk.com

Heading to Koko for the first time after its refurbishment is a bit like going to your favourite squat party and finding they've removed the tower of beer cans and put in an Axminster carpet. When Charlie Chaplin used to tread the boards here in the early twentieth century it was probably pretty nice but to most gig-goers it's best known either as punk haven The Music Machine (in the 70s) or splendidly grotty rave dive and occasional indie disco The Camden Palace (in the 80s and 90s). It shut in 2004 but reopened later in the year with a look that owes a little to Moulin Rouge and a lot to the desire of owners Mint to turn it into the kind of place that corporations throwing big parties will feel just as happy in as gig-goers. They've had some stick for this but I can't see why. If they'd left it as the sticky-carpeted shell that it was people would have complained about that, too. The intimate alcoves and gorgeous bordello-red bars that honeycomb the levels above the dancefloor look amazing and nights here will undoubtedly see the same foreign exchange student debauchery that they always did. It's just that now they're desperately trying to get off with each other underneath, wait for it, the largest mirror ball in Europe.

LARK IN THE PARK

ADDRESS: 60 Copenhagen Street, Islington, London N1 0JW
PHONE: 020 7278 5781
OWNER: Sami
DOOR PRICE: £5-£6
PRICE OF THEIR MOST POPULAR PINT OR BOTTLE: £2.70 (pint of Stella Artois)
OPENING HOURS: 11.00am - 2:00am (Thurs / Fri / Sat). Other nights vary.
FOUNDED: 2004 as a music venue (1930s as a pub)
CAPACITY: 175 (plus an extra 80 in the garden for parties in a marquee)
SOME ACTS WHO'VE PLAYED HERE: No one well known yet although legendary Beatles producer George Martin's latest prodigy Charity appeared.
WHAT'S ON? New rock bands (Tues) Acoustic nights (Weds) Private parties and bookings by outside promoters (Thurs / Fri / Sat).
WHO SHOULD BANDS TALK TO ABOUT PLAYING? Send demos to Sami at the above address.
WHAT'S THE SOUND LIKE? OK.
WHAT'S THE DEAL FOR BANDS? Bands generally keep the door unless they're dealing with an independent promoter.
HOW DO WE GET THERE? It's between King's Cross and Angel tube stations. From King's Cross turn left and left again and head down York Way which runs parallel with the station. Copenhagen Street is a few hundred yards down on the right. The venue is on the corner of Barnard Park on the left.
website: www.larkinthepark.co.uk

With its stage incongruously stuck at one end of a homely, wood-panelled pub and the PA stacked awkwardly on the end of the bar Lark

In The Park looks like it should be one of those places where old codgers who nearly got signed in the 70s warble Don McLean covers at annoying volume when you're trying to have a quiet pint. Wisely or not, though, the owner seems to be trying to establish it as somewhere a little cooler than that. I say wisely because the last time I went two of the bands hadn't shown up, proving the precariousness of setting up a business based on dealing with musicians – never known for their reliability. So far Lark In The Park is a long way from establishing itself as a rival to the venues a mile or so north west in Camden, or east in Islington. If they're going to make a name for themselves they need to get a promoter who can do what the Windmill has done in Brixton or The Luminaire in Kilburn.

LOCK 17

ADDRESS: 11 East Yard, Camden Lock, NW1 8AB
PHONE: 020 7428 5929
MANAGER: Matt Ward
DOOR PRICE: usually £7 - £15
OPENING HOURS: varies but they have a license to 2.00am. Bands are usually 7.30pm – midnight but some play later.
PRICE OF THEIR MOST POPULAR PINT OR BOTTLE:
£2.70 for a pint of Stella Artois
FOUNDED: 70s
CAPACITY: 487
SOME ACTS WHO'VE PLAYED HERE: The Stone Roses, The Fall, U2, The Thrills, Tom Vek, Ed Harcourt.
WHAT'S ON? At weekends there's the comedy club Jongleurs, there are various club nights in the week plus an 'unplugged' night on Wednesdays and occasional visits from bigger bands. There are plans to re-start the 'Jam Monologue' club for unsigned bands on the last Sunday of the month.
WHAT'S THE SOUND LIKE? Good.

Rock London 2006

WHO SHOULD BANDS TALK TO ABOUT PLAYING? Most gigs are put on by outside promoters but to play Jam Monologue send demos to Hanna Pettersson at the address above (check website for details).

WHAT'S THE DEAL FOR BANDS? For Jam Monologue in the past bands were paid £1 per person they brought. Otherwise it's by negotiation.

HOW DO WE GET THERE? Nearest tube station is Camden. Turn right out of the station up Camden High Street and turn left just past the canal into Camden Lock place.

website: www.lock17.com

The compromise between the old, grimy Camden and the new one of corporate money is best represented by Lock 17. It used to be known as Dingwalls and it was a typically scuzzy, often unbearably hot sweatpit of a venue right next to the once-filthy canal that sidles discreetly out of Camden and off through Regent's Park. They've cleaned the canal up now though and Lock 17 have established a nice bar on the roof looking out across it and a successful comedy club, Jongleurs, downstairs. Amongst all this bands still play, although not as often as they used to, and it's a pretty good place to watch them. From the bar you can look across the heads of the crowd to the stage because there are steps down to a lower level right in front of it and the atmosphere is a strange mixture of old style rock venue and corporate comedy club. It's pretty clear that the latter is the owner's priority but venues of this size are fairly thin on the ground in Camden so it would be good to see them putting more bands on again.

THE LUMINAIRE
ADDRESS: 311 High Road, Kilburn, NW6 7JR
PHONE: n/a
PROMOTER: Andy Inglis
DOOR PRICE: usually £5
OPENING HOURS: Tues – Thurs (8.00pm – midnight), plus other nights occasionally.
PRICE OF THEIR MOST POPULAR PINT: £2.90 (pint of Carling)
FOUNDED: March 2005
CAPACITY: 270
SOME ACTS WHO'VE PLAYED HERE: Redjetson, Cazals, Dead Fly Bukowski, Dive Dive, Editors, Vincent Vincent and the Villains, The Rakes.
WHAT'S ON? Residential nights Tuesday, Wednesday and occasional Thursdays plus outside promotions Take The High Road (indie / rock - 1st Thurs of the month); Hedonistic (indie / rock - 2nd Thurs); Nylon Or Bust (three comedians followed by two bands – 3rd Thurs); Club Everlasting (indie / rock 1st Weds).
WHAT'S THE SOUND LIKE? Good.
WHO SHOULD BANDS TALK TO ABOUT PLAYING? Send an MP3 to Andy at info@theluminaire.co.uk or, failing that, a demo to PO Box 50735, London, NW6 7ZA
WHAT'S THE DEAL FOR BANDS? On the Residential nights the promoter takes 25% of the door and the rest is split three ways with the three bands depending on how many people they bring, how far they've come, whether they steal the towels etc.
HOW DO WE GET THERE? It's just down the road from Brondesbury mainline station, about five minutes from Kilburn tube station (Jubilee line) and about 12 minutes from Kilburn Park tube station (Bakerloo line). From Kilburn Station turn right on to Kilburn High Road and it's a little way along on your right next to and above The Kilburn Bar.
website: www.theluminaire.co.uk

Like a lot of the better new venues in London The Luminaire is something of a rescue job. With its chilly blue lighting and 80s decor it looks like it's designed for the worst kind of pseudo-sophisticated bar culture. As you come up the stairs and walk into what looks like a pool hall without the pool tables it doesn't seem to have much more atmosphere than the bland Kilburn Bar downstairs. And, at weekends, it does revert to type as a kind of bar / disco but on Tuesdays, Wednesdays and Thursdays it hosts a similar line-up to unofficial sister venue The Windmill in Brixton. Promoter Andy Inglis claims that the venue's popularity with new bands stems from being nice to them and "giving them towels". Whether that will last or not (knowing bands they probably nick the towels) it's good to see rock coming back to Kilburn. Like Camden it used to be a big Irish area and that always seems to mean live music but since the Kilburn National Ballroom lost its license it seems to have been in short supply round here. A lot of venues are friendly and a lot are professionally run but The Luminaire is one of the few that manage both at once.

MADAME JO JO'S

ADDRESS: 8-10 Brewer Street, W1F 0SE
PHONE: 020 7734 3040
MANAGER: Paajoe Gaskin
DOOR PRICE: £5 - £38 (the top price is for cabaret nights, including food)
PRICE OF THEIR MOST POPULAR PINT OR BOTTLE: £3.50 (for a bottle of Grolsch etc)
OPENING HOURS: 7.00pm – 3.00am
FOUNDED: 60s
CAPACITY: 180
SOME ACTS WHO'VE PLAYED HERE: Kings Of Leon, Scissor Sisters, Murderdolls, Joy Zipper, Dresden Dolls, Sheep On Drugs.

Rock London 2006

WHAT'S ON? White Heat (Tues) for indie / art rock / punk; comedy (Weds); Electrogogo (monthly Thurs – dance legend Mark Moore's night); Glitz (monthly on Thurs electro-rock); Keb Darges Legendary Deep Funk (Fri); Groove Sanctuary (Sat – soulful house etc); The Indelible Marker (Sun – hip-hop)

WHAT'S THE SOUND LIKE? Good.

WHO SHOULD BANDS TALK TO ABOUT PLAYING? Send demos to Paajoe at the address above or contact the promoters direct.

WHAT'S THE DEAL FOR BANDS? negotiated with promoters.

HOW DO WE GET THERE? It's in the heart of Soho in between Piccadilly, Oxford Circus, Tottenham Court Road and Leicester Square tube stations.

website: www.madamejojos.com

Sometimes what venue a band books is purely down to chance and logistics but sometimes it can say a lot about them. This is certainly the case at Madame Jo Jo's. If managers of big bands are straight on the phone to the Royal Albert Hall when they want a little class by association then it's Madame Jo Jo's they call when they're looking for a certain kind of sophisticated, knowing sleaze. For about 30 years it was almost exclusively known as 'London's Premier Drag Queen Cabaret Club' but recently they've broadened their appeal with new club nights, occasional 'burlesque' dancers and much more frequent appearances from live bands. It's also very popular with record launch parties and other corporate events and you can see why. Once inside it's like being in a Martini advert from the 60s with heavy drapes and shameless scarlet walls. Just the place to convince journalists that they're seeing something daring and innovative, especially if somebody else is picking up the wallet-frightening Soho bar prices. More recently, though, live music has become such a major part of its business that even bands who probably don't deserve it are getting to borrow the facade of glamour that only Madame Jo Jo can provide.

THE MARQUEE

ADDRESS: 1 Leicester Square, WC2H 7NA
PHONE: 0870 444 6277 (venue, not promoters)
PROMOTER: Sarah and Matthew at Plum Promotions
DOOR PRICE: usually £6 (£5 concessions)
PRICE OF THEIR MOST POPULAR PINT OR BOTTLE:
£3 (pint of Fosters)
OPENING HOURS: usually 7.00pm – 11.00pm
FOUNDED: 1958, if you accept that someone can buy history. 2003 if you don't.
CAPACITY: usually 100 for bands downstairs but on level three there's a balcony which takes it up to 500 and the newly opened Level 5 bar is 400.
SOME ACTS WHO'VE PLAYED HERE: The Ordinary Boys, Tom Vek, Magic Numbers, Ash, Rilo Kiley, The Bees, Goldie Lookin Chain.
WHAT'S ON? Bands most nights a week.
WHAT'S THE SOUND LIKE? Good.
WHO SHOULD BANDS TALK TO ABOUT PLAYING? Send demos to Sarah or Matthew at Plum Promotions (check website for guidelines)
WHAT'S THE DEAL FOR BANDS? No deposit or pay to play but they need to bring about 40 people to get paid (by negotiation).
HOW DO WE GET THERE? Nearest tube is Leicester Square. It's on the North West corner (the far corner on your right as you enter the Square from the station).
website: www.plumpromotions.com (promoters)

The Marquee is such a resonant brand in London's rock scene that the name has now been shamelessly stuck to five different venues: an Oxford Street Jazz club (1958-1964), a Wardour Street rock club (1964-1988), a Charing Cross venue that's now a crappy pub (1988-1996), the swanky venue that's now the Islington Academy (2002 – 2003) and this old dance club in Leicester Square (2004- ?). It was the second version that made the place's name with legendary visits from all the big names of the 70s. Once that failed most people would have decided that the brand was finished but club owners are made of sterner stuff. They know from the booze prices they can get away with that gig-goers are basically pretty simple and they've continued trying to convince us that various, entirely different venues, are actually part of the same long thread in rock history. Still, the Leicester Square version is an OK venue in its own right. The acoustics in the main room are good and the high ceilings allow a huge, atmospheric cloud of cigarette smoke to hang above the stage. The ambience when I last went seemed somewhat contaminated by the grim meat market vibe of the surrounding clubs but if there's someone playing who you want to see then there's no reason to avoid it.

THE MEAN FIDDLER

ADDRESS: 157 Charing Cross Road, WC2H 0EL.
PHONE: 020 7434 9592
MANAGER: Julie Friel
DOOR PRICE: Varies between £7-£25 depending on the band.
PRICE OF THEIR MOST POPULAR PINT OR BOTTLE:
£3.30 for a can of Grolsch
OPENING HOURS: 6.30pm - 11.00pm usually, 3.30am (Fridays) 4.00am (Saturdays). 2.00am (at Jump Off, every other Monday)
FOUNDED: About 20 years ago as a music venue.
CAPACITY: 800 - 1000
SOME ACTS WHO'VE PLAYED HERE: Gang Of Four, Pulp, The Cranberries, Placebo, Queens Of The Stone Age, Turbonegro, The Subways.
WHAT'S ON: Bands seven nights a week plus clubs afterwards: Rock (Fridays) Metal Hammer magazine's metal, punk and rock night with bands. Frog (Saturdays) indie and alternative bands with more of the best new bands. The Jump Off (every other Monday) hip-hop club with 8-Mile

style battling etc. Check website for updates and more details.
WHAT'S THE SOUND LIKE? Excellent
WHO SHOULD BANDS TALK TO ABOUT PLAYING? n/a all done through promoters.
WHAT'S THE DEAL FOR BANDS? n/a
HOW DO WE GET THERE? It's just round the corner from Tottenham Court Road tube station on Charing Cross Road (follow the signs from the station). It's also on the main bus route for many buses that terminate at the nearby Trafalgar Square.
website: www.meanfiddler.com

Until fairly recently this venue was called 'The LA2' and the ambience is almost identical to that of its larger sister venue The London Astoria next door. The main difference is that instead of the seating area that's upstairs at The Astoria here there's a balcony and a bar where, oddly, you can watch the bands play through a window that muffles the sound. I suppose the idea is that if the band sound good above the music industry chit-chat and through a pane of plexi-glass you know it's worth sprinting downstairs. Once you get there the atmosphere is much less London than at lot of the capital's venues, by which I mean the crowds are younger, more enthusiastic and less inclined to stand around talking about record label mergers. Instead they rush to the front and spend the night struggling to avoid getting pushed off the dancefloor which is, for some reason, raised about a foot off the floor. Like most other venues that have changed names you'll find some refuseniks don't acknowledge this as 'The Mean Fiddler' – for them that name will always be reserved for a, now closed, venue on Harlesden High Street which helped kick-start the ever burgeoning Mean Fiddler empire. Not everybody loves the organisation, notably the local council who've made occasional attempts to shut the whole complex down, but this place makes a fine flagship.

METRO

ADDRESS: 19-23 Oxford Street, W1R 2DN
PHONE: 020 7437 0964
PROMOTER: Paul Tunkin
DOOR PRICE: usually £6 - £10
PRICE OF THEIR MOST POPULAR PINT OR BOTTLE:
£3 (bottle of Becks) + special offers on some club nights.
OPENING HOURS: 7.00pm – 3.00am (Mon – Fri) 7.00pm – 4.00am (Sat).
FOUNDED: As a club approximately 30 years ago. As a venue 2000
CAPACITY: 175
SOME ACTS WHO'VE PLAYED HERE: The Darkness, Scissor Sisters, Yeah Yeah Yeahs, The Kills, The Libertines
WHAT'S ON? Bands most nights plus clubs starting at 11.00pm. Electric Dreams (80s new romantic / goth etc - Mon); Beautiful People (nu-metal, emo & skate punk - Tues); Hysteria (Indie / New Wave / hair metal / electro - Weds); The Bunker (post-punk / rock 'n' roll – Thurs); Bedrock (indie / alt / retro – Fri); Blow Up (60s garage, Latin, rock'n'roll – Sat)
WHAT'S THE SOUND LIKE? good.
WHO SHOULD BANDS TALK TO ABOUT PLAYING? Send demos to Metro Gigs, c/o Blow Up, PO BOX 4961 London W1A 7ZX England. (read guidelines on the website first)
WHAT'S THE DEAL FOR BANDS? by negotiation.
HOW DO WE GET THERE? It's next door to Tottenham Court Road tube station on Oxford Street.
website: www.blowupmetro.com/

At the beginning of the 90s this small basement venue at the scummier end of Oxford Street was briefly the centre of what the music press dubbed 'The Scene That Celebrates Itself', giving it a possible claim on the birthplace of two movements: shoegazing and britpop. Never mind that the first fizzled out without making much of an impact and the second was only represented by members of Blur drinking themselves into a stupor in the days when they couldn't be bothered to stagger up to Camden. Even now it still looks like it's waiting for some kind of scene to stumble in and declare the place its headquarters. The walls are lined with mirrors making it the ideal place for celebrating oneself but also adding to a slightly oppressive atmosphere. The ambience is pitched in that very indie place somewhere in between a feather boa and a battered leather jacket ie: grimy, seedy, anti-glamour. Indeed since the Blow Up organisation took Metro over in 2001 it has successfully reinvented itself as something like a small piece of indie Camden stranded on Oxford Street. Anywhere else in London this would be a pretty horrible venue but in the tawdry West End it remains something of an alternative, albeit somewhat stagnant, oasis.

MONTAGUE ARMS

ADDRESS: 289 Queens Road, New Cross, SE14
PHONE: 020 7639 4923
PROMOTERS: Fear Of Music and various others.
DOOR PRICE: usually £3-4
PRICE OF THEIR MOST POPULAR PINT: £2.50 (Stella Artois)
OPENING HOURS: Opening hours are a little mysterious and variable but it's generally agreed it doesn't open Mon – Weds.
FOUNDED: unclear.
CAPACITY: 150 (approx)
SOME ACTS WHO'VE PLAYED HERE: Clor, Zongamin, Death From Above 1979, Gang Of Four, The Young Knives. Pink Floyd supposedly played in the 70s and Shane McGowan, Mark E Smith and Nick Cave once had an impromptu jamming session here in 1989 after an NME interview.
WHAT'S ON? There are bands on most Fridays and some Thursdays.

WHAT'S THE SOUND LIKE? OK

WHO SHOULD BANDS TALK TO ABOUT PLAYING? You could try contacting Fear Of Music fearofmusic436@yahoo.co.uk or come down on one of the other promoters' nights with a demo.

WHAT'S THE DEAL FOR BANDS? Negotiable but most of the New Cross promoters have a reputation for being band-friendly.

HOW DO WE GET THERE? Nearest tube station is New Cross Gate on the East London line. Turn right out of the station and head down New Cross Road, Queens Road branches off on the left and Montague Arms is a short way down on the right. Queens Road Peckham mainline station is also near (ten minutes from London Bridge).

website: none.

The Montague Arms is probably the strangest venue in this book. It looks like it was furnished by Uncle Bulgaria waking up after a long night on the sauce and drunkenly ordering the Wombles to "bring me...stuff!' Apparently it used to be owned by a taxidermist, which would explain the stuffed animals dotted about the place, but there's also an ocean theme with ships' wheels and broken boats on the walls. On Sunday afternoons the ancient bar staff turn out a very well-regarded roast which is enjoyed by coach loads of Belgian tourists passing though on their way back home after daytrips to London, on Saturdays a blind organist and his band play, and on most Fridays and some Thursdays the full force of the New Cross 'scene' descends on the place. It came into its own when the Paradise Bar (now the Six String) temporarily shut and it's been gaining in popularity ever since. With its big stage and unique atmosphere it looks like it should have been one of South London's best venues forever but in fact it's fairly recently been revitalised by the resurgence of live music in South East London.

NAMBUCCA

ADDRESS: 596 Holloway Road, N7
PHONE: 020 7263 6939
PROMOTER: Jay McCallister
DOOR PRICE: free (sometimes £1 Fri / Sat)
PRICE OF THEIR MOST POPULAR PINT OR BOTTLE:
£2 (pint of Carling)
OPENING HOURS: 6.00pm – midnight.
FOUNDED: 2004 (as Nambucca) 19th century as a pub.
CAPACITY: 100 (so far)
SOME ACTS WHO'VE PLAYED HERE: Babyshambles, Vincent Vincent And The Villains, The Holloways, Mystery Jet.
WHAT'S ON? Jenny Jenny Presents (new indie bands - Sat) Heartwarm (Country / Americana - Fri) Sensible Sundays (open mic night – Sun) occasional bands other nights. Check website for details.
WHAT'S THE SOUND LIKE? OK.
WHO SHOULD BANDS TALK TO ABOUT PLAYING? Send demos etc to info@hollowayroad.co.uk
WHAT'S THE DEAL FOR BANDS? Payment (if any) by negotiation. No deposit or pay to play.
HOW DO WE GET THERE? It's in between Archway and Holloway Road tube stations. From Holloway Road turn left, cross over and it's a short walk on the right. From Archway turn right down Holloway Road and it's a short walk on the left.
website: www.hollowayroad.co.uk

This bit of London seems to special in grandiose statements. The Archway Tavern just down the road claims, somewhat ludicrously, to be 'North London's Premier Music Venue' and the Nambucca confidently boasts that it's "The Best Pub In North London". Maybe, if you're only comparing it to the other, generally horrible, pubs along Holloway Road.

For a long time this venue was one of them, as its many Sellafield-esq changes of name, attest (The Swagman's Rest, The Cock and now Nambucca) but the landlord let a group of well-connected promoters live upstairs and, despairing of the general emptiness, they're trying to make it into a proper music venue. This is to be heartily applauded because the place itself isn't that bad. It's a big pub with a small, triangular stage in one corner and a number of comfy leather sofas and armchairs that look like they were reclaimed from a skip dotted around. The only major flaw, then, is that at the time of writing they have a ludicrously small official capacity of only 100 (it could fit three times that). This puts the unfortunate doorman in the position of having to turn people away even though they can see through the big plate windows that the back of the pub is completely empty. Until they sort this (and we're promised the capacity will be doubled eventually) it's not a place to make a special journey to but the promoters do seem to have an ear for good bands.

NOTTING HILL ARTS CLUB

ADDRESS: 21 Notting Hill Gate, W11 3JQ
PHONE: 020 7598 5226
OWNER: David McHugh
DOOR PRICE: free before 8pm in the week (£5 after). Free Saturday afternoons 4.00pm – 8.00pm. Sunday afternoons before 6.00pm. £6 before 11.00pm Fri / Saturday nights, £8 after 11.00pm.
PRICE OF THEIR MOST POPULAR PINT OR BOTTLE:
£2.95 (bottle of Lapin)
OPENING HOURS: 6.00pm – 1.00am (Mon-Weds) 6.00pm – 2.00am (Fri) 4.00pm – 2.00am (Sat) 4.00pm – 1.00am (Sun)
FOUNDED: 1997
CAPACITY: 218
SOME ACTS WHO'VE PLAYED HERE: The Hives, The Darkness, Black Rebel Motorcycle Club, The Libertines, Louie, Art Brut, Special

Needs, Pure Reason Revolution.

WHAT'S ON? Art, music and film from Scandinavia, the Mediterranean and the far east (Mon); DJs or electronica from Mute Records (Tues); Death Disco (Weds); Edgy hip-hop and R&B (Thurs); Inspiration Information (soul / funk breakbeats, etc – Fri) RoTa Sessions (live indie etc – Sat afternoons); Global party music (Sat nights); Underdog (Deep House - Sun afternoons).

WHAT'S THE SOUND LIKE? Alright, not brilliant.

WHO SHOULD BANDS TALK TO ABOUT PLAYING? The website has a list of contact details for the promoters of the different nights (Death Disco don't accept unsolicited demos).

WHAT'S THE DEAL FOR BANDS? Depends on promoter (by negotiation)

HOW DO WE GET THERE? At Notting Hill tube station take the exit with the sign towards 'Kensington Church Street' and it's about two hundred yards on your right.

website: www.nottinghillartsclub.com/

The Notting Hill Arts Club is a tiny reminder of the days when this part of London used to be cool. Well, alright, it's still probably quite cool if you've got lots of money or you're around for the Notting Hill Carnival but any area that gets a Julia Roberts romantic comedy named after it must immediately suffer a severe hit on its hipdom. Endearingly the club is barely visible from the street as though ducking away from the rich newcomers to the area. After an unnecessarily thorough search by the doormen you go down some steps and into a basement that looks like it comes straight out of some too-cool-to-be-true film about Swinging London. There's a large circular bar in the middle and, in the great tradition of basement clubs, there's usually only about 30 people who can see at any one time but the atmosphere is excellent. The main thing that's made the club in recent years is the decision of ex-Creation Records boss Alan McGee and friends to locate their excellent Death Disco club here on Wednesdays and the famous Rough Trade shop's arrival for the free ROTA club on Saturday afternoons. As well as all this there's also all the 'Art' that you'd expect, with various exhibitions giving the place an atmosphere that subtly reminds you that, like, rock clubs are culture, too, you know.

ON THE ROCKS
ADDRESS: 25 Kingsland Road E2 8AA
PHONE: n/a
MANAGER: Byron Evans
DOOR PRICE: from £3 (with a flyer) to £10
PRICE OF THEIR MOST POPULAR PINT OR BOTTLE:
£3 (pint of Grolsch)
OPENING HOURS: 8.00pm – midnight (Weds), 8.00pm – 2.00am (Thurs), 10.00pm – 2.00am (Fri – Sat), 10.00pm – 1.00am (Sun).
FOUNDED: 1994 as a DJ bar. 2001 as a regular venue.
CAPACITY: 250
SOME ACTS WHO'VE PLAYED HERE: White Stripes, The Darkness, The Glitter Band (without Gary).
WHAT'S ON? 1-2-3-4 Records and Pure Groove Presents (new bands – Thurs); Trailer Trash (house, electro, electroclash etc – Fri); Coast To Coast (ska / Reggae – alternate Sat); Machine (electroclash etc – alternate Sat).
WHAT'S THE SOUND LIKE? OK
WHO SHOULD BANDS TALK TO ABOUT PLAYING? Send demos to the management or get in touch with 1-2-3-4 or Pure Groove.
WHAT'S THE DEAL FOR BANDS? negotiable.
HOW DO WE GET THERE? Nearest tube is Old Street Station. Take exit 2 and turn left down Old Street past the Holiday Inn Express hotel and Kingsland Road is on your left. On The Rocks is past Catch and Herbal on the left.
website: none

In London, as in most other cities, the number, quantity and quality of bars and clubs often seems to be directly in proportion to how ugly the surroundings are. This is certainly true of Kingsland Road Shoreditch, the grimy corner of East London where you'll find On The Rocks. It looks like the road to hell (it's worse than that, it's actually the road to Hackney) but it's just round the corner from the excellent 333 Club while the hugely cool Herbal Club and Catch Bar are diagonally opposite. On The Rocks is grungier and, appropriately, rockier than the rest of the area. With fronds of purple tinsel around the walls it's obviously going for a kind of seedy glamour but it's much more successful in the former than the latter. For a certain kind of modern rock'n'roll band with a Libertines fetish, too many Ramones albums and maybe a battered synthesiser to add a touch of modernity it's easy to see why it would seem like a home from home. And, as there are an awful lot of those kind of rock'n'roll bands around in East London right now, its future should be secured.

PLEASURE UNIT

ADDRESS: 359 Bethnal Green Road, Bethnal Green, E2 6LG
PHONE: 020 7729 0167
OWNER: Nick
DOOR PRICE: occasionally free - up to £6
PRICE OF THEIR MOST POPULAR PINT OR BOTTLE:
£2.80 (pint of Grolsch)
OPENING HOURS: 7.30pm until midnight Sunday to Thursday, until 2.00am Friday & Saturday.
FOUNDED: 2001 as The Pleasure Unit. It was built in 1862 as The White Hart Pub.
CAPACITY: 150
SOME ACTS WHO'VE PLAYED HERE: Pete Doherty, The Buff Medways, Metro Riots, Little Barrie.
WHAT'S ON? Mostly indie, rock and punk but other new music does

get an airing. Mondays it's currently Sawdust Caesars for the fastest rising new bands (four a night). Tues, Weds, and Thurs is 'Don't Forget Your Bass Amp' for more new bands. Then there are various club nights (check website for details).

WHAT'S THE SOUND LIKE? Good

WHO SHOULD BANDS TALK TO ABOUT PLAYING? Send demos to Nick at the address above or send a brief biog to bands@pleasure-unitbar.com

WHAT'S THE DEAL FOR BANDS? Negotiable. New bands generally get £1-£2 per person if they bring 30+ people but the owners say they don't let bands they like go out of pocket.

HOW DO WE GET THERE? From Bethnal Green Tube station turn left on to Bethnal Green Road and it's less than half a mile on the right. Liverpool Street and Old Street stations are both a bit less than a mile away. website: www.pleasureunitbar.com

The Pleasure Unit is another of those East London venues that gets away with looking like a student squat because they know the locals like it like that. This isn't meant as a criticism. Bethnal Green Road is a pretty horrible part of town and the fact that someone's managed to turn the grotty frontroom of a pub into something like this is great. Before becoming the Pleasure Unit it was a DJ bar for a time and before that a gay bar called 'The Cock And Comfort' but it looks like an old man's pub that's been gutted in about five minutes with a few 60s-style pictures and slogans hastily tacked up. It's built its reputation on the number of good new bands that have emerged in the area recently and, unlike a lot of venues, they have a small hardcore of regulars who will turn up even if there isn't an act they know playing. Bands coming from less 'edgy' parts of the world might feel like they need an armoured car to take them past the scary youths hanging around outside McDonalds but, such is the pace of change in the area, that by the time this book comes out there'll probably be a Malaysian-Swiss fusion bar next door and we'll all be lamenting the loss of Bethnal Green's 'unique' ambience.

PURPLE TURTLE

ADDRESS: 61-65 Crowndale Road, Camden Town, NW1 1TN
PHONE: 020 7383 4976
MANAGER: Rachelle Budgen
DOOR PRICE: From £3 - £6
PRICE OF THEIR MOST POPULAR PINT OR BOTTLE: £2.90 (pint of Kronenbourg)
OPENING HOURS: midday to midnight (Sun - Thurs) midday to 2.00am (Fri – Sat)
FOUNDED: 1998
CAPACITY: 285
SOME ACTS WHO'VE PLAYED HERE: The Pipettes, Do Me Bad Things, The Departure.
WHAT'S ON? Spineshaker (for new bands, Mondays and Tuesdays) plus various club-nights including Stay Beautiful for glam-indie etc on the first Friday of the month.
WHAT'S THE SOUND LIKE? Good
WHO SHOULD BANDS TALK TO ABOUT PLAYING? Send demos to Spineshaker, 152 Wightman Road, N8 0BD or contact the promoters directly.
WHAT'S THE DEAL FOR BANDS? Depends on the promoter but Spineshaker pay £1 for each person after the first five.
HOW DO WE GET THERE? It's virtually opposite Mornington Crescent tube station (Northern Line). Turn right and you'll see it a short way down Crowndale Road.
website: www.purpleturtlebar.com

Anyone would look a little bit scuzzy standing just across the street from Koko but, although Purple Turtle might not have the plush decor of its neighbour, that's probably the point. Part of a small chain of so-called 'alternative' bars it looks like a slightly wacky, goth spaceship with 'turtle' themed light-fittings, metal walkways leading to a cramped balcony upstairs and a reasonably large stage at right angles to the main bar. Once it was well known for a famously debauched drum and bass club that took place on Sunday nights but since 2003 they've been trying to attract more bands with more and more success. The place comes into its own when the excellent Stay Beautiful club comes to visit. Anyone not wearing either fishnet stockings and / or copious amounts of eye-liner might feel a bit out of place but the club fits Purple Turtle's 'Star Wars' bar ambience perfectly. The chain's website promises that there will be "no tedious bastards telling you you've drunk to much" and, while you might not want to bring that up with the bouncers while they're throwing you out, the bar does a good job of living up to its 'alternative' image. It was announced recently that it was to be re-christened The Buzzard and taken over by the people who run the Buffalo Bar in Islington. At the time of writing this hasn't actually happened but, even if it does, the place will no doubt continue its focus on live music.

RHYTHM FACTORY

ADDRESS: 16-18 Whitechapel Road, Shoreditch E2
PHONE: 020 7375 3774
MANAGER: Alex Ling
DOOR PRICE: Usually £5 (weekdays) £5 - £10 (weekends)
PRICE OF THEIR MOST POPULAR PINT: £2.80 (bottle of Becks)
OPENING HOURS: 11.00am – 1.00am (weekdays) 11.00am – 5.00am (weekends)
FOUNDED: 2000
SOME ACTS WHO'VE PLAYED HERE: The Libertines, Dizzee Rascal, Towers Of London, James Taylor Quartet, Dogs, The Paddingtons, Groove Armada.
CAPACITY: 400
WHAT'S ON? Bands most nights plus Bring Your Own Poison (rock),

Let Them Eat Gak (indie) both generally monthly. A Spoonful Of Poison (open mic night - every other Monday). Check website for details.
WHAT'S THE SOUND LIKE? OK
WHO SHOULD BANDS TALK TO ABOUT PLAYING? Send demos and brief biog FAO Spoon at the address above.
WHAT'S THE DEAL FOR BANDS? Negotiable but new bands will need to bring about 30 + people to get paid.
HOW DO WE GET THERE? It's in between Aldgate East and Whitechapel tube stations. From Whitechapel turn right out of the station and it's a short walk on your left.
website: www.rhythmfactory.co.uk

One of the more endearing things about the painfully cool people who live in this bit of East London is that they seem unable to walk past a derelict building without immediately deciding to turn it into some kind of bar, cafe or club. I say endearing because, for all everyone takes the piss out of their 'ironic' hairstyles it should be remembered that before the arty types arrived in the 90s this area was best known for Jack The Ripper and he only managed to murder eight people (child's play by modern standards). The Rhythm Factory, like much of this area, was derelict for ten years before the present owners took it over and in typical Shoreditch fashion they've made a virtue out of its gritty, industrial appearance. This is a polite way of saying that the actual building is a bit of a dump but that people seem to like it like that. At the front is a café selling cheapish Thai food and out the back are two more bars, one a surprisingly big room where they put the bands on. It's almost too big, particularly with the not terribly impressive PA that they've got set up, but, as Whitechapel is still established as a centre for artistic talent, there's no shortage of good bands willing to play here. The Libertines were just one band signed after a gig here and it's certain they won't be the last.

ROCK GARDEN

ADDRESS: Rock Garden, 6/7 The Piazza, Covent Garden, WC2E 8HA
PHONE: 020 7257 8626
PROMOTER: Lisa @ Platform Music (for Sunday afternoon new bands showcase)
DOOR PRICE: £4 (before 7pm on Sundays) £5 afterwards. Check website or listings for other nights.
PRICE OF THEIR MOST POPULAR PINT OR BOTTLE: £2.50 (bottle of Grolsch)
OPENING HOURS: 11.00am - 2.00am (Sun) 5pm - 3.00am (Mon - Thur) 5.00pm - 4.00am (Fri - Sat)
FOUNDED: mid 70s.
CAPACITY: 250
SOME ACTS WHO'VE PLAYED HERE: U2, Talking Heads, The Stranglers, The Manic Street Preachers, Wet Wet Wet, The Orb, Dire Straits
WHAT'S ON? New bands on Sunday afternoons (folk, funk, soul, pop, indie and the lighter end of rock) a 'Battle Of The Bands' on 7.30pm-10pm Sunday nights (club till 2.00am) and a 'Best of Platform' showcase on the last Wednesday of every month. Various club nights the rest of the week (check website for details).
WHO SHOULD BANDS TALK TO ABOUT PLAYING? Send demos to Lisa of Platform Music at the address above.
WHAT'S THE SOUND LIKE? OK
WHAT'S THE DEAL FOR BANDS? If you bring 40+ paying punters you get paid 50% of the door.
HOW DO WE GET THERE? Nearest tube is Covent Garden. Turn right out of the station, cross Floral Street and the Rock Garden is on the piazza facing the covered market.
website: www.rockgarden.co.uk

Apparently around 30,000 bands have played at the Rock Garden in the last thirty years. In the nineties, although bands still played, the name became somewhat inappropriate as they became better known for offering greasy, tourist trap food upstairs, and the popular and acclaimed Gardening Club for dance music downstairs. Recently, though, they've reinvented themselves again. The restaurant's been revamped and dragged upmarket and the club are tentatively experimenting with live music again. So far this just means that on Sunday afternoons they hand the club over to promoters Platform who put on an eclectic mixture of indie, funk, soul, pop, folk and singer-songwriters. If you're after anything edgy, dangerous and uncompromising then this probably isn't the right place to come but then again who is on a Sunday afternoon? The atmosphere, with drapes gently billowing from the ceiling and tables dotted in front of the stage, is more conducive to sophisticated conversations about European cinema and polite applause than rock'n'roll mayhem but new bands could hardly hope to find a friendlier, more supportive audience to play for. Although this may well change later when the venue run a 'Battle Of The Bands' night.

ROYAL ALBERT HALL

ADDRESS: Kensington Gore, London SW7 2A
PHONE: 020 7589 3203
CHIEF EXECUTIVE: David Elliott
DOOR PRICE: anything from £5 - £100
PRICE OF THEIR MOST POPULAR PINT OR BOTTLE:
£3.30 (can of Carling)
OPENING HOURS: varies.
FOUNDED: 1871
CAPACITY: 5,222
SOME ACTS WHO'VE PLAYED HERE: Bob Dylan, Nina Simone, Spiritualized, The Who, Robbie Williams, Coldplay, Eric Clapton, Cream
WHAT'S ON? Wide range of classical music, ballet, etc plus several

major rock and pop acts a year. It's also open for tours in the daytime.
WHAT'S THE SOUND LIKE? Good.
WHO SHOULD BANDS TALK TO ABOUT PLAYING? n/a (all arranged through outside promoters).
WHAT'S THE DEAL FOR BANDS? n/a
HOW DO WE GET THERE? Nearest tube stations are South Kensington (District, Circle and Piccadilly lines) and Kensington High Street (District and Circle lines). It's sign-posted from both and there's a map on the website.
website: www.royalalberthall.com

In its time the Royal Albert Hall has hosted everything from Sumo Wrestling (the first time in 1,500 years a 'Grand Basho' was held outside Japan) to the first speaking engagement of Mr Stanley after he found the famous Dr Livingstone ("I presume") in Africa. Basically anybody who thinks they'll benefit from playing somewhere terribly, terribly posh is desperate to play here. It was built as a spin-off of Britain's Great Exhibition in 1851. The result is one of those buildings built in a classical style to try and not-very-subtly suggest to everyone that we were the new Roman Empire. The Empire may be long gone but it's still an amazing place to go on the rare occasions when anybody decent plays here. You sit in relatively plush seats that form a semi-circle in front of the stage and, in the cheaper circle, look down on the performers from vertiginous heights. Prince Albert, whose idea the building was, is best known now for the unpleasant piercing named after him so it's a good job the poor old, erm, chap has something a little grander to boast about.

THE ROYAL STANDARD
ADDRESS: 1 Blackhorse Lane, E17 6DS
PHONE: 020 8503 2523
MANAGER: Amanda Crighton.
DOOR PRICE: usually £5

PRICE OF THEIR MOST POPULAR PINT OR BOTTLE:
£2.30 (pint of Carling)
OPENING HOURS: 8.30pm – 1.00am
FOUNDED: 1892 as a pub, 1950s as a music venue.
CAPACITY: 300
SOME ACTS WHO'VE PLAYED HERE: Iron Maiden, Suzi Quatro, Phil Lynott, The Zombies, Sugarcoma, Wilko Johnson.
WHAT'S ON? Tribute bands Fri / Sat, new bands Thursdays, outside promoters / hire-outs Weds.
WHAT'S THE SOUND LIKE? Good.
WHO SHOULD BANDS TALK TO ABOUT PLAYING? Mark demos FAO Amanda, at The Standard Music Venue (address above). Check website for guidelines.
WHAT'S THE DEAL FOR BANDS? Negotiable.
HOW DO WE GET THERE? It's directly opposite the Blackhorse Road tube station on the Victoria Line
website: www.standardmusicvenue.co.uk

When the managers of The Royal Standard told this book that their venue would close if London was awarded the Olympics, it seemed about as likely as it closing because aliens wanted to build a car park in the garden. Astonishingly, though, this bit of East London is playing host to the games and the bar at the Royal Standard is (alright, very very approximately) at the point where the 100 metre runners will leave the blocks. Of course the landlord could always suggest that they sprint along the stage (it's almost big enough) but, sadly, this Victorian pub is ear-marked for demolition. Not that the place has been a hotbed of new music in recent years. Most of the week it's devoted to tribute bands but they do put on new stuff on Thursdays and the last Friday of every month. The most famous act to come from this neck of the woods were, of course East 17, who loyally named themselves after their deeply unfashionable postal code. But as everything in London seems to be

Rock London 2006

shifting East, with clubs closing in Camden and opening in Shoreditch, maybe this bit of the city could be the next, unlikely 'New Hoxton'. Ironically the new money pouring into the area may make this more likely and, at the time of writing, The Royal Standard's management are looking into the possibility of re-establishing the club at a new venue nearby.

SCALA
ADDRESS: 275 Pentonville Road Kings Cross, N1 9NL
PHONE: 020 7833 2022
EVENTS CO-ORDINATOR: Sasha Heeney
DOOR PRICE: Usually from £5 - £15
PRICE OF THEIR MOST POPULAR PINT OR BOTTLE:
£3 (can of Red Stripe)
OPENING HOURS: when bands are on it's usually 7.00pm – midnight, clubs at the weekend are 10.00pm – 3.00am.
FOUNDED: 1920 (as a cinema) re-opened as a club in 1999.
CAPACITY: 1,000
SOME ACTS WHO'VE PLAYED HERE: British Sea Power, DJ Vadim, Super Furry Animals, Death From Above 1979, Black Rebel Motorcycle Club, Fischerspooner, Rilo Kiley, Editors.
WHAT'S ON? Popstarz (gay indie night every Friday); Club Rampage (Kerrang's monthly rock night on Saturdays).
WHAT'S THE SOUND LIKE? OK
WHO SHOULD BANDS TALK TO ABOUT PLAYING? n/a all done through outside promoters.
WHAT'S THE DEAL FOR BANDS? n/a
HOW DO WE GET THERE? It's virtually opposite King's Cross Station. Turn left out of the station and on to Pentonville Road. Scala is also adjacent to the Thameslink train station on Pentonville Road.
website: www.scala-london.co.uk/scala

As you'll be able to tell from its fantastic, palatial exterior The Scala is another venue that was originally built as a cinema in the days when they thought that the invention of pictures that, like, moved wouldn't be enough on its own to drag people out of their houses. We owe its current incarnation as a cutting-edge club to an ill-advised decision in 1993 to illegally show Stanley Kubrick's 'A Clockwork Orange'. The Scala Cinema Club lost its court battle, went into receivership and it wasn't until 1999 that it reopened in some style with four floors, three bars and spanking clean wooden floors everywhere after a grant of some £35 million from the EU. It may not be as cool as the 1974 Scala, when the likes of Iggy Pop, Hawkwind and Gary Glitter appeared at all-nighters, or the 1979 Scala when they bizarrely changed it into an ecology exhibition called a 'Primatarium' (me neither) where the stalls of the cinema were reconstructed to resemble a forest, but the new version does put on some great club nights. It hasn't yet caught the imagination as a mainstream live venue in quite the same way, possibly because the sound always seems slightly echoey for rock bands but the atmosphere is always good.

SHEPHERD'S BUSH EMPIRE

ADDRESS: Shepherd's Bush Empire, Shepherds Bush Green, W12
PHONE: 020 8354 3300
MANAGER: all enquiries to owners, McKenzie Group
DOOR PRICE: usually £12 - £25 approx
PRICE OF THEIR MOST POPULAR PINT OR BOTTLE:
£2.95 (pint, can or bottle of Carling).
OPENING HOURS: usually 7.00pm – midnight.
FOUNDED: 1903
CAPACITY: 2000 (1278 when all-seated)
SOME ACTS WHO'VE PLAYED HERE: David Bowie, The Kinks, Duran Duran, The Rolling Stones, The Who, Oasis, Kylie Minogue, Sheryl Crow, Blondie, Bob Dylan, Bjork, Iron Maiden, Coldplay, Destiny's Child.

WHAT'S ON: Big name bands several nights a week.
WHAT'S THE SOUND LIKE? Excellent.
WHO SHOULD BANDS TALK TO ABOUT PLAYING? n/a
WHAT'S THE DEAL FOR BANDS? n/a
HOW DO WE GET THERE? Nearest tube station is Shepherd's Bush. From the Central Line station turn right and walk across Shepherd's Bush Green. It's on the far corner of the green. From the Hammersmith and City line branch turn left and then, almost immediately, go straight on down Shepherd's Bush Road parallel with the green.
website: www.shepherds-bush-empire.co.uk

Shepherd's Bush Empire should be familiar to most people who grew up in Britain. Although it started life as a popular music hall it was bought by the BBC in 1953 and used to film long-running programmes like 'Wogan' and 'That's Life'. The clock in the foyer is still set at five to five – the time legendary children's programme Crackerjack aired. This doesn't make it sound like a particularly exciting venue but, although it does have a slightly cosy, teatime atmosphere it's one of the best seated venues in London. Although they do have a standing area at the front unless you buy your ticket early you're likely to find that you're sitting halfway up what feels like a vertical cliff. This layering of seated areas means that the atmosphere is more concentrated, and the view is better than some other venues. The main reason why most fans end up coming here, though, is because most bands end up coming here at some point when they're not quite big enough for Brixton Academy but slightly too big for the Forum. Reason enough.

SIX STRING BAR

ADDRESS: 460 New Cross Rd, London, SE14 6TJ
PHONE: 020 8692 1530
MANAGER: John Bundy
DOOR PRICE: £3

PRICE OF THEIR MOST POPULAR PINT OR BOTTLE:
£2.70 (pint of Kronenbourg)
OPENING HOURS: 11.00am – 12.00 midnight
FOUNDED: It was built as a pub, The Royal Albert, well over a hundred years ago but it's best known as The Paradise Bar. In its most recent incarnation as The Six String Bar it reopened in May 2005.
CAPACITY: 250
SOME ACTS WHO'VE PLAYED HERE: Bloc Party, Athlete, Art Brut, Squeeze, Charlie Chaplin.
WHAT'S ON? blues / folk (Tues); new indie (Thurs) Lava club (ambitious 'pop' (indie is a dirty word apparently) - Fri).
WHAT'S THE SOUND LIKE? OK
WHO SHOULD BANDS TALK TO ABOUT PLAYING? Try the website below for Lava nights or send demos to John Bundy at the address above to pass on to relevant promoter.
WHAT'S THE DEAL FOR BANDS? Depends on the promoter but for Lava (Friday nights) bands can expect to get roughly £1 for each person they bring if they bring 23 or more. However, they try and cover petrol costs for bands who've travelled.
HOW DO WE GET THERE? Nearest tube station is New Cross. Turn left out of the station on to New Cross Road and it's a big white building less than a hundred metres down on the right.
website: none (www.lovepeacemusic.clara.net for promoters)

"That's what I love about New Cross," a bass player announced after technical problems at one recent Six String Bar gig, "you know that somebody in the crowd will have a bass drum pedal in their pocket." Bands playing here shouldn't necessarily rely on this but The Six String is one of those venues where at least half the crowd look like they're in bands so borrowing equipment from the crowd is always going to be a possibility. "The CBGBs of SE14" is the promoters' tongue-in-cheek description of the place and it's not entirely inaccurate. If anywhere can claim to be the headquarters of the much-discussed New Cross scene it's here. It might look a bit like a student union bar at the brightly lit back half, partly because most of the punters probably attend the nearby Goldsmiths University, but the front half looks like a South London version of Notting Hill Art Club's 'Death Disco'. There's a slightly more relaxed, less self-consciously cool atmosphere but the people congregating underneath the slowly spinning glitterball have the same unshakable confidence that they're at the coolest place in the world right now. In reality that honour probably goes to The Montague Arms, about half a mile down the road, but the Six String comes close.

SOUND

ADDRESS: Swiss Centre, Leicester Square, W1D 6QF
PHONE: 020 7287 1010
PROMOTER: Helen
DOOR PRICE: £5 (on Wednesday) other nights vary.
PRICE OF THEIR MOST POPULAR PINT: £2.50 (for a bottle of Budweiser at the Chu-Bar Club, other nights it's more)
OPENING HOURS: 7.30pm – 3.00am
FOUNDED: 1997 (as Sound)
CAPACITY: 600
SOME ACTS WHO'VE PLAYED HERE: Coldplay (regularly before they were signed), The Darkness.
WHAT'S ON? The Chu-Bu club on Wednesdays puts on five unsigned bands, usually indie / rock, followed by an indie club. They also put on 'Sound Unplugged' with acoustic nights from bigger bands in the café on Tues and Thursday. The rest of the week is your usual West End club stuff (R&B, chart pop, disco, latin, etc) and other promoters occasionally put bigger bands on. Check website for more details.
WHAT'S THE SOUND LIKE? Excellent.

Rock London 2006

WHO SHOULD BANDS TALK TO ABOUT PLAYING? Send demos to PO BOX 10349, London NW1 9WJ or e-mail Helen: info@thetalentscout.co.uk
WHAT'S THE DEAL FOR BANDS? Unspecified but they're not likely to make any money unless they bring 50+ people.
HOW DO WE GET THERE? From Leicester Square tube station you can't miss the Swiss Centre on the other side of the square.
website: www.soundlondon.com

Sound is an expensive and swanky looking club on the corner of Leicester Square much prized by the organisers of corporate parties for being a bit less tacky than some of the other big clubs in the area. This isn't saying much. At weekends and on most nights of the week they offer an alcopop-sodden crowd the usual mix of chart cheese but on Wednesday they've recently started a new club called Chu-Bu for live music. Although it's a cold, sterile place entirely lacking in atmosphere I suppose for a lot of new bands it must be nice to play a big room with a sound rig which is vastly superior to anything they're likely to have experienced before. The only problem with new music nights they've put on in the past is that nobody turns up except friends of the bands and that's rarely enough people to fill the large capacity. They also put on showcases for big bands and maybe that's a more sensible use of the space. There's never going to be much atmosphere if you've got 50 or so people in a club big enough for 600.

SPITZ
ADDRESS: The Spitz, 109 Commercial St, Old Spitalfields Market, E1 6BG
PHONE: 020 7247 9747
MANAGER: Martin Wissenberg
DOOR PRICE: free - £15
PRICE OF THEIR MOST POPULAR PINT OR BOTTLE:

£3 (pint of Heineken)
OPENING HOURS: 7.00pm – midnight (Mon –Weds) 7.00pm –1.00am (Thurs – Sat) 4.00pm - 10.30pm (Sun)
FOUNDED: 1996
CAPACITY: 250
SOME ACTS WHO'VE PLAYED HERE: British Sea Power, Dick Dale, Turin Brakes, Damo Suzuki, Kings Of Convenience, Bloc Party, Cat Power, Ed Harcourt, James Yorkston.
WHAT'S ON? Live music upstairs seven nights a week. Plus restaurant downstairs and art gallery.
WHAT'S THE SOUND LIKE? good
WHO SHOULD BANDS TALK TO ABOUT PLAYING? Send demos to Martin Wissenberg at the address above.
WHAT'S THE DEAL FOR BANDS? Negotiable but bands probably need to be able to bring at least 50 people to get paid (no deposit or pay to play).
HOW DO WE GET THERE? Nearest tube is Liverpool Street. Take the Bishopsgate exit and turn left. Cross over the road and head down Brushfield Street on the right until you reach Spitalfields Market. The Spitz is on the corner furthest from you. (Map on website).
website: www.spitz.co.uk

The Spitz has a more sophisticated atmosphere than most East London venues. There's a fancy restaurant downstairs as well as an art gallery while the stage in the venue upstairs is illuminated by candlelight. This can mean that the atmosphere is slightly precious but it does make a nice change from venues that think providing two kinds of lager is a major customer service. In keeping with this ambience they tend to put on bands who appear to a relatively mature audience so you get singer songwriters, folk, jazz and other genres that seem to inspire people to sit on the floor. When David Bowie came here he apparently commented that it was 'very bohemian' which is true, I suppose, although depending on how he said it it's hard to work out whether that was supposed to be a compliment or not. 'Nice' would be a more accurate description and believe it or not that is meant as a compliment. The venue sits on the corner of the famous Spitalfield's Market which was for a long time threatened with demolition. Luckily, for once art, or at least tourism, won out over the encroaching financial district and The Spitz seems secure.

ST MORITZ

ADDRESS: 159 Wardour St, Soho, W1
PHONE: 020 7437 0525
OWNER: Arman Loetscher
DOOR PRICE: £5 before 11.00pm, £7 after
PRICE OF THEIR MOST POPULAR PINT OR BOTTLE:
£3.00 (bottle of Amstell)
OPENING HOURS: 10.00pm-3:30am (Gaz's Rockin' Blues - Thurs)
FOUNDED: 1960
CAPACITY: 120
SOME ACTS WHO'VE PLAYED HERE: Deep Purple, The Sweet, Joe Strummer (in his pre-Clash band the 101ers), The Trojans (Gaz Mayall's band)
WHAT'S ON? Gaz's Rockin' Blues every Thursday. Indie club Friday, rock club Saturday.
WHAT'S THE SOUND LIKE? Good.
WHO SHOULD BANDS TALK TO ABOUT PLAYING? Send demos marked Gaz's Rockin' Blues to the address above.
WHAT'S THE DEAL FOR BANDS? Bands get at least £50, usually more.
HOW DO WE GET THERE? It's between Tottenham Court Road, Leicester Square, Oxford Circus and Piccadilly Circus tubes. From Tottenham Court Road tube head down Oxford Street and Wardour Street is a short way down on your left. St Moritz is on the right.
website: www.gazrockin.com

Wardour Street used be one of the most popular places to come for live music in the 60s and 70s when legendary venue The Marquee (a name now borrowed by a new club on Leicester Square) was located on the street. After The Marquee kicked out at about 11.00pm the punters and, very often, many of the bands used to come down the road to the St Moritz. It's been here since 1960, as has the owner Arman Loetscher who can proudly claim to have been the subject of a song written by Joe Strummer in his 101ers days: 'Sweety Of The St Moritz'. The lyrics are stuck to the wall as you walk down the stairs into the basement and it doesn't seem to bother Sweety that it was apparently written about the 101ers struggle to get paid! These days the venue is a slightly more humble establishment with the nice Swiss Restaurant upstairs the subject of more attention, although the long running Gaz's Rockin' Blues night on Thursdays still has a major cachet among blues fans. In its time at Gossips venue it hosted some huge names and while the basement here is a little smaller it's still going strong.

THE TELEGRAPH
ADDRESS: 228 Brixton Hill, Brixton SW2 1HE
PHONE: 020 8678 0777
PROMOTER: Alex Berger
DOOR PRICE: from free - £7 (bands usually £5)
PRICE OF THEIR MOST POPULAR PINT OR BOTTLE:
£2.50 (pint of Stella)
OPENING HOURS: The pub opens at 12.30pm. Club bit's open till 12.30am Sun, 2.30am (Mon – Thurs), 6.00am (Fri / Sat).
FOUNDED: 1874
CAPACITY: 300 for bands (650 in total)
SOME ACTS WHO'VE PLAYED HERE: The Clash, Bob Marley, Stereo MCs, The Others, The Noisettes, Lynton Kwesi Johnson, Basement Jaxx, Ozric Tentacles.

Rock London 2006

WHAT'S ON? Sunday Supplement (up to eight bands 4.00pm – 11.00pm); Motel Fetish (rock / punk – Weds); various indie bands (Thurs); occasional bigger name bands other nights. Clubs (house / breakbeats / etc) weekends.

WHAT'S THE SOUND LIKE? Excellent.

WHO SHOULD BANDS TALK TO ABOUT PLAYING? Send demos to Alex Berger at the address above or e-mail to alex@thebrixtontelegraph.co.uk

WHAT'S THE DEAL FOR BANDS? £1 for each person they bring as long as they bring 10 or more people.

HOW DO WE GET THERE? From Brixton tube turn left and it's about ten minutes walk up Brixton Hill.

website: www.thebrixtontelegraph.co.uk

The brilliant plan of a lot of venues in the 00s is to be everything to everybody all at once. This is certainly the case at The Telegraph which is a hybrid of DJ Bar, club and Thai restaurant with enough of the old man's pub ambience left intact just in case the fickle clubbers ever leave and they need to get the original Irish regulars back. Right at the top of Brixton Hill a fair walk from the tube station they obviously have to work to get people up here but then as the place has been a staging post for Morse Code operators and a naval hospital in its time that's probably always been the case. It's best known either as "the home of The Clash" because Joe Strummer made his live debut here with the 101ers in 1974 and played regularly ever after, or as the home of Basement Jaxx's hugely popular 'Rooty' parties. At the moment, although the club side is still doing well, they're trying to re-establish it as a credible place for guitar bands. In recent years they haven't pulled in the quality line-ups of the much more modest Windmill just down the road but it's worth keeping an eye on the listings.

TROUBADOUR CLUB

ADDRESS: 263-7 Old Brompton Road, SW5 9JA
PHONE: 020 7370 1434
PROMOTER: Amanda Glynn
DOOR PRICE: £5
PRICE OF THEIR MOST POPULAR PINT OR BOTTLE: £3 (bottle of Budvar)
OPENING HOURS: 8.00pm – 2.00am (Thurs / Fri / Sat). 8.00pm – 12.30am (Sun – Weds) in the club. Café is open 9.00am – midnight.
FOUNDED: 1954
CAPACITY: 120 (in the club)
SOME ACTS WHO'VE PLAYED HERE: Jimi Hendrix, Joni Mitchell, Bob Dylan, Paul Simon, Led Zeppelin, Elvis Costello, Babyshambles, Clayhill, Yeti.
WHAT'S ON? The Sessions (new, unsigned bands – Weds); 3 bands a night (Thurs / Fri); (alternate short film / poetry nights – Mon); private hire other nights.
WHAT'S THE SOUND LIKE? Good.
WHO SHOULD BANDS TALK TO ABOUT PLAYING? Send demos to Amanda at the address above.
WHAT'S THE DEAL FOR BANDS? They're expected to bring at least 10 people and the door split is negotiable. The Sessions bands aren't paid but they are given dinner.
HOW DO WE GET THERE? It's two minutes from West Brompton tube station and about four minutes from Earls Court tube.
website: www.troubadourclub.co.uk

The Troubadour opened in the 50s as a coffee bar when coffee was establishing itself as the drink of choice for turtle-necked beatniks everywhere. Satirical magazine 'Private Eye' was first produced and distributed here, the Campaign For Nuclear Disarmament kicked off with early 'Ban

The Bomb' meetings here and the radical folk movement of the early '60s made the place home. It might have had its zenith when Bob Dylan played his debut UK gig here but, forty years later, it's still going strong although that might be more to do with the acclaimed café upstairs than the music venue. Downstairs in the club the atmosphere is nice enough but there's very little sense of the excitement that must have been generated when Led Zeppelin dropped in to jam following gigs at nearby Earl's Court. It's mostly seated and if you're left standing the atmosphere can seem a little awkward and uncomfortable. Maybe that's just because it's a very grown-up place with the music seemingly intended as a backdrop to civilised conversation. There's nothing wrong with this but you'd like to think that Bob was granted a bit more attention. Still, 50 years after the last coffee house boom, The Troubadour has more claim to the spirit of those times than the likes of Starbucks.

ULU
(UNIVERSITY OF LONDON UNION)
ADDRESS: Malet Street, Bloomsbury, WC1E 7HY
PHONE: 020 7664 2085
MANAGER: Laurie Pegg
DOOR PRICE: From £2 to £15
PRICE OF THEIR MOST POPULAR PINT OR BOTTLE:
£2.80 (pint of Grolsch).
OPENING HOURS: n/a
FOUNDED: 1955
CAPACITY: 828 (big room) 400 (small room) (pre-refurbishment)
SOME ACTS WHO'VE PLAYED HERE: Nirvana, Keane, Coldplay, And You Will Know Us By The Trail Of Dead, Travis.
WHAT'S ON? Bands several times a week.
WHAT'S THE SOUND LIKE? Good.
WHO SHOULD BANDS TALK TO ABOUT PLAYING? Send a demo to DEMOS at the address above.

WHAT'S THE DEAL FOR BANDS? by negotiation.
HOW DO WE GET THERE? Nearest tube stations are Goodge Street and Warren Street. From Goodge Street turn left down Tottenham Court Road and then take Torrington Place on the right. Malet Street is the fourth street on the right.
website: www.ululive.com

To a lot of indie bands students must occupy a similar role to that that sheep play in the life of lonely mountain farmers: a longterm meal ticket and a potential shag in one convenient package. In many towns the only big venue is the student venue and although this obviously isn't the case in London, the ULU (pronounced Yoo-Loo) is still popular, even with regular folks, for the (relatively) cheap beer and for the uncomplicated combination of a cavernous room and some good bands. That's why there must have been consternation in some quarters when the ULU shut in June 2005 but, after refurbishment, it's reopening in September. It's fair to say a little refurbishment has been in order for quite a while. When empty the big hall always looked like it was just waiting for the next amateur performance of 'God Spell' to start. For all that Universities like to portray themselves as cool, freewheeling, fast-living institutions, when you walked through this one's yellow corridors you couldn't help but realise that it's just school with a subsidised bar attached. Still, even if they can't make it look any cooler there's bound to be more bands following famous alumnus Coldplay's Chris Martin from the sticky floors and into the big time.

THE UNDERWORLD

Address: 174 Camden High Street, NW1 0NE
Phone: 020 7482 1932
Promoter: various in-house, AL Douglas for unsigned bands.
Door price: varies from £3 - £15
Price of their most popular pint or bottle: £3.30 (pint of Carlsberg Export)
Opening hours: usually 7.00pm – 11.00pm for bands then, at weekends or other club nights, punters are kicked out to make way for clubbers.
Founded: early 90s
Capacity: 500
Some acts who've played here: At The Drive-In, Mastodon, Frank Black, Hole, J Mascis, The Offspring, Placebo, Radiohead, Sepultura, Sheryl Crow, Smashing Pumpkins, Soundgarden, Suede, The Darkness.
What's on? Bands virtually every night plus clubs: Pump Up The Volume (80s 11.00pm-3.00am Fri); Silver (indie 11.00pm – 3.00am Sat); Nasin (punk / metal 11.00pm –2.00am Weds) Kung Fu (soul / hip-hop 9.00pm – 3.00am 3rd Tuesday of the month). Check website for updates.
What's the sound like? Very loud.
Who should bands talk to about playing? New / unsigned bands should send demos to Live & Xposed, AL Douglas, PO BOX 47544, London N14 4YT (check website for guidelines or promoters website www.wildplum.co.uk)
What's the deal for bands? negotiable.
How do we get there? It's right behind Camden Tube Station (take the Kentish Town Road exit).
website: www.theunderworldcamden.co.uk

The Underworld is below what is, according to the sign on the door, "probably the biggest pub in London" but don't let that put you off.

Although The World's End is much too big to be likeable the Underworld, for all its faults, is probably the premier place to see new metal and punk bands in London. If you were going to build a music venue then it would be worth coming here to see exactly what not to do but it does sort of work. The first thing you'll notice is that to get down to the front you have to first venture down a disconcertingly sloping floor and then down some narrow steps which become very treacherous if you arrive late and have to get past dozens of people. Then, approximately 30 seconds after the last bands come off stage you'll find brusque security guards ushering you out to make way for another set of paying clubbers. Which always seems a bit greedy. Despite all this, though, if you like metal or any of the harder end of rock The Underworld's always going to be the place to come. Maybe it's the fact that when it's rammed to capacity and everyone's trying to get down the front it has a ferociously rock'n'roll ambience which few other venues can match.

THE VENUE
ADDRESS: 2 Clifton Rise, New Cross, SE14 6JP
PHONE: 0208 692 4077
PROMOTER: Richard Evans
DOOR PRICE: from £3 to £15
PRICE OF THEIR MOST POPULAR PINT OR BOTTLE: £2.90 (pint of Stella Artois)
OPENING HOURS: In the main club it's 9.00pm-4.00am (Fri), 9.00pm-4.30am (Sat). In the basement on new music nights it's 9.00pm-2.00am.
FOUNDED: 1989 (as The Venue) before that it was The Harp.
CAPACITY: 200 (in the basement) 600 (in the main hall)
SOME ACTS WHO'VE PLAYED HERE: Pulp, Oasis, Blur, Radiohead (in the old days). The Pipettes, Lady Sovereign, Punish The Atom, The Fucks, The Violets, Neil's Children (in the basement since new bands started playing again).
WHAT'S ON? Tribute bands every weekend plus, on occasional Fridays,

new bands in the basement bar with the 'I Swear I Was There' and 'Fear Of Music' nights.

WHAT'S THE SOUND LIKE? Good.

WHO SHOULD BANDS TALK TO ABOUT PLAYING? Tribute bands should get in contact with Richard Evans at the address above. 24 Records, Angular Records, and Fear Of Music put on new bands monthly in the basement. Try fearofmusic436@yahoo.co.uk.

WHAT'S THE DEAL FOR BANDS? Negotiable.

HOW DO WE GET THERE? From New Cross Gate station (on the East London line) turn left on to New Cross Road and it's on the corner of Clifton Rise about a hundred yards down the road.

website: www.thevenuelondon.com/

To indie fans of a certain age The Venue is the Darth Vader of the music scene. It opened under this name in 1989 and became one of the most popular venues to see the first wave of Britpop bands but, in 1995, the East London tube line closed for a lengthy period of refurbishment and, as north London's indie fans couldn't be bothered to traipse down anymore, the owners made the decision to turn to the dark side: tribute bands. And, give them their due, they've done a good job because The Venue has become synonymous with them. Despite the fact that they've got six separate rooms, until recently they nearly all seemed to be devoted to various flavours of cheese. This might have made sense a couple of years ago but with New Cross acclaimed as "the new Hoxton" in various over-excitable quarters the time seems right for The Venue to return to its roots. That's what much celebrated local labels 24, Angular and promoter Fear Of Music think, anyway, and they've started putting on nights here in the Venue Basement: a Moroccan themed mock-boudoir of stone arches, low ceilings, drapes and big cushions. It's entirely separate to the The Venue proper so if you get bored with edgy, modern stuff there'll always be a Shakin' Stevens double waiting next door.

WATER RATS

ADDRESS: 328 Grays Inn Road, London WC1X 8BZ
PHONE: 020 7336 7326 (promoters only)
PROMOTER: Sarah and Matthew at Plum Promotions
DOOR PRICE: usually £4 - £8
PRICE OF THEIR MOST POPULAR PINT OR BOTTLE:
£2.80 (pint of Stella Artois)
OPENING HOURS: 8.00am - 11.00pm (doors usually 7.00pm for bands)
FOUNDED: nineteenth century as a pub.
CAPACITY: 200
SOME ACTS WHO'VE PLAYED HERE: Bob Dylan, Oasis, The Pogues, Beta Band, Mogwai, The Darkness.
WHAT'S ON? Four bands most nights.

WHAT'S THE SOUND LIKE? Good.
WHO SHOULD BANDS TALK TO ABOUT PLAYING?
WHAT'S THE DEAL FOR BANDS? No deposit or pay to play but probably need to bring at least 30 people (payment by negotiation)
HOW DO WE GET THERE? From King's Cross station walk down the main road in front of you and to the left, where the Kentucky Fried Chicken is. The club is approximately 400 metres down the road on the left hand side.
website: www.plumpromotions.co.uk (promoters)

Any small venue that's been around for a few years can reel off a list of big names who took their first steps there. Not many can match the Water Rats, though, which boasted an early performance by Bob Dylan in 1962, the Pogue's debut in the early 80s and Oasis's first headline gig in 1994. Maybe it's significant that all three vocalists have a certain nasal quality to their voices - The Ear Nose And Throat Hospital is right next door. Or, alright, maybe not. Back when Mr Dylan played here the place was called the Pinder Of Wakefield and it was the centre of Britain's folk scene. Then in the 80s the room upstairs became the headquarters of a charitable organisation called The Grand Order Of Water Rats and changed its name. If you ever see Paul Daniels, Roger de Courcey or any other luminary of 70s Britain hanging around you'll know why; they're all members, along with dozens of other forgotten heroes of light entertainment. The Water Rats itself is very likeable both as a pub and a venue. It doesn't seem to have quite the same cachet as it once did but it's a more comfortable place to watch music than, say, the Barfly. Just try and find a view without a pillar in the way. And if you find yourself right in front of the speakers at least you won't have to go far to get your ears sorted out.

WEMBLEY ARENA

ADDRESS: Stadium Way, Wembley, HA9 0DW
PHONE: 0870 060 0870 (tickets) 0208 902 8833 (office)
MANAGER: n/a
DOOR PRICE: usually £30 - £40
PRICE OF THEIR MOST POPULAR PINT OR BOTTLE: £3 (pint of Carling)
OPENING HOURS: usually 6.30pm – 11.00pm
FOUNDED: 1934
CAPACITY: 10000 (seated in the temporary Pavilion), 7000 (in the exhibition hall – 4000-5000 seated).
SOME ACTS WHO'VE PLAYED HERE: The Beatles, Duran Duran, The Offspring, Queen, Alice Cooper, Frankie Goes To Hollywood, Kylie Minogue.
WHAT'S ON? Huge bands most months.
WHAT'S THE SOUND LIKE? Used to be very variable but with luck it will be improved with the refurbishment.
WHO SHOULD BANDS TALK TO ABOUT PLAYING? n/a
WHAT'S THE DEAL FOR BANDS? n/a
HOW DO WE GET THERE? Nearest tube is Wembley Park (Zone 4) on the Metropolitan & Jubilee Line - eight-minute walk. From the station cross the road and take the steps down onto Olympic Way, cross Engineers Way and the Pavilion is on your left. For Wembley Show Hall turn right out of the station following Empire Way. Turn left into Stadium Way. Wembley Stadium railway station is also nearby and Wembley Central tube station (Bakerloo line). Map and directions on the website below.
website: www.whatsonwembley.com

The name 'Wembley' enjoys a strange position in the British psyche. The famous Football Stadium was the scene of England's only World Cup victory in 1966, various pitch invasions by angry / jubilant Scottish fans whenever they came down to play and of course the FA Cup Final every year. For all these sentimental reasons, then, very few people complained that it was a bit of a crap-hole stuck out in an inaccessible suburb of West London. Still, at least the Stadium had a bit of character. The adjacent Arena was a notoriously awful venue with bad sound, no atmosphere and ludicrous ticket prices. Luckily, since they've bulldozed the Stadium and started building an even bigger, swankier one on the same site the owners have had the grace to be somewhat embarrassed by the horribleness of its little brother and it's presently closed for extensive refurbishment until 2006. In the meantime they're still putting on gigs at a temporary all-seater pavilion out the back and rockier stuff will happen in the old Exhibition hall. The main focus of refurbishment is a new 'Arena Square' in between the Arena and the Stadium. It's going to be modelled, in size and style, on Leicester Square with cinemas, bowling alleys etc. This and the fact that the new Wembley Way is going to be lined with shiny new shops suggests that the main focus of the place is still going to be squeezing as much money as possible out of people but maybe they'll start doing something to earn it now.

WEST ONE FOUR
ADDRESS: 3 Northend Crescent, West Kensington W14 8TG
PHONE: 020 7603 7006
MANAGER: Derren Miller-Price
DOOR PRICE: £5-£15
PRICE OF THEIR MOST POPULAR PINT OR BOTTLE:
£3.25 (pint of Stella Artois)
OPENING HOURS: 12.00pm – midnight (in the week and Sun), 12.00pm – 1.00am (Fri) 9.00am – 1.00am (Sat).
FOUNDED: 1988 (as a music venue)
CAPACITY: 300

SOME ACTS WHO'VE PLAYED HERE: Busted, Mica Paris, Jamiroquai, Feeder, Brand New Heavies, Robert Palmer, Ocean Colour Scene, Labi Siffre.

WHAT'S ON? Mon 'The Original Singer-Songwriters' night, twice monthly on Tuesdays is the demo night for unsigned bands, Thursdays promoters Feed Me Music put on rock / indie bands, and Fri / Sat / Sun there are various indie and rock bands.

WHAT'S THE SOUND LIKE? Excellent

WHO SHOULD BANDS TALK TO ABOUT PLAYING? Main promoters are Feed Me Music and Orange Promotions. For the unsigned, 'demo nights' send a demo by e-mail to Derren at info@westonefour.com

WHAT'S THE DEAL FOR BANDS? Currently they take a deposit of £80 from small bands, which is refundable if they bring at least 16-20 people. Feed Me Music pay £2 per person for every person after the first 20, Orange Promotions currently pay £2 per person once they reach 20, including that 20. Bigger bands can hire the venue. Check with manager or promoters for updates.

HOW DO WE GET THERE? It's very near West Kensington tube station, turn right on to North End Road and you'll see it on the corner of North End Crescent. It's also near Baron's Court tube station and there's a map on the website.

website: www.westonefour.com

The blue lights on the roof of West One Four illuminate the street outside like a fridge left open in a dark kitchen. A similarly chilly atmosphere inside might explain why this place isn't somewhere that bands with pretensions to a different kind of coolness tend to play. This is despite the fact that it's got a sound system of such power and clarity that it would make pretty much every other venue of a similar size blush in shame. Inside it looks like its designed for some kind of cabaret with tables in front of the stage and an imposing bar which runs along one wall flogging booze at the usual exorbitant Kensington prices. It's a fair bet that most people you see here can 'play' in a muso sense but, unfortunately for the owners, most cool bands and most fans prefer to spend their time in converted crack dens in the East End or stinkholes in Camden. For any new bands who think their destiny is to sell out arenas then playing here could at least be good practise because the atmosphere is very similar. This, obviously, is not meant as a compliment.

THE WINDMILL
ADDRESS: 22 Blenheim Gardens, Brixton, SW2 5BZ
PHONE: 020 8671 0700
PROMOTER: Tim Perry
DOOR PRICE: £3
PRICE OF THEIR MOST POPULAR PINT OR BOTTLE:
£2.80 (pint of Kronenbourg)
OPENING HOURS: 5.00pm – 12.00am in the week, 12.00pm – late at weekends (varies).
FOUNDED: 2001 as a venue, 70s as a pub.
CAPACITY: 170
SOME ACTS WHO'VE PLAYED HERE: Calexico, The Rakes, Icarus Line, The Crimea, Art Brut, Bloc Party, Mclusky, 5-6-7-8s, Kurt Wagner (of Lambchop).
WHAT'S ON? Three bands a night, seven days a week except for one Saturday a month where they host the much acclaimed 'People's Republic Of Disco' – where punters bring their two favourite records and the management spin them randomly throughout the night. Check website for updates and more details.
WHAT'S THE SOUND LIKE? OK
WHO SHOULD BANDS TALK TO ABOUT PLAYING? Send demos to Tim Perry at the address above.

WHAT'S THE DEAL FOR BANDS? Bands split the whole of the door money between them depending on how many people they bring.
HOW DO WE GET THERE? From Brixton tube turn left and it's about seven minutes walk up Brixton Hill. Blenheim Gardens is on the right and the pub is about 50 yards down the street.
website: www.windmillbrixton.co.uk

It's often been said that you should never drink in pubs with a flat roof. That's because they tend to be concrete bunkers stuck on the end of grim housing estates for the sole purpose of soaking the occupants in booze so thoroughly that they don't notice the urban squalor all around them. The Windmill is the exception that proves the rule. From the outside it looks like an estate pub that's been captured by hippies and that may not be far from the truth but the nice thing about it is that it still maintains a local flavour even while maintaining a line-up of great new bands that would be the envy of every other small venue in South London. It makes you wonder why other clubs can't do this: cheap tickets, reasonable booze prices, friendly atmosphere and, bonus, they even seem to clean the toilets occasionally. It doesn't have the sound system or the facilities of other local venues but they've proved that that doesn't matter too much if you get the right bands and the right crowd. The Windmill could easily become the victim of its own success, it can't be easy to run a venue in such a residential area, but for now it's probably the most likable venue of its size in London.

Venue Addresses

12 Bar Club
12 Bar Club, Denmark Street, London, WC2H 8NL
Andy Lowe (promoter)
Tel: 020 7916 6989 (office)
12barclub@btconnect.com

93 Feet East
Truman Brewery, 150 Brick Lane, London E1 6QN
Sean Hitchings (live music promoter)
Tel: 020 7247 3293
sean@93feeteast.co.uk

100 Club
100 Oxford Street, W1D 1LL
Jeff Horton (owner)
Tel: 020 7636 0933
info@the100club.co.uk

Ace Café
Ace Corner, North Circular Road, Stonebridge, London, NW10 7UD
Mark Wilsmore (owner) Linda (music booker)
Tel: 020 8961 1000
linda_acecafelondon@lineone.net

Ain't Nothing But Blues Bar
20 Kingly Street, W1B 5P
Tel: 020 7287 0514

ALEXANDRA PALACE
Alexandra Palace Way, Wood Green, London N22 7AY
Tel: 020 8365 4316
chris.gothard@alexandrapalace.com (marketing)

AMERSHAM ARMS
388 New Cross Road, New Cross, London SE14 6TY
Tel: 020 8692 2047
Philip Martin (bar manager) or promoter Titch Turner
info@catapultclub.co.uk
titch.van@btopenworld.com

ARCHWAY TAVERN
1 Archway Close, N19 3TX
Tel: 020 7272 2840
Landlord: Patrick
patricko66@lycos.co.uk

ASTORIA
157 Charing Cross Road, London WC2H 0EL
Tel: 020 7434 0403
(Mean Fiddler Group)
management@londonastoria.co.uk
Mark Ellicot (manager)

BARBICAN
Barbican Centre
Silk Street
London EC2Y 8DS
Tel: 020 7638 4141
Thomas Hardy (music programming)
thardy@barbican.org.uk

BARDEN'S BOUDOIR
38-44 Stoke Newington Road
Andrew Hickson - 07812595529, or Andrew Doig – 07708 656633 (promoters)
Umit Moroglu – 0777 6066921 (manager)

BARFLY
49 Chalk Farm Road, London, NW1 8AN
Tel: 020 7691 4244
london.info@barflyclub.com
jeremy.ledlin@channelfly.com

THE BEDFORD
77 Bedford Hill, Balham, SW12 9HD
Tel: 020 8682 8940
Tony Moore (manager)
info@thebedford.co.uk

BETSEY TROTWOOD
56 Farringdon Road, EC1R 3BL
Tel: 020 7336 7326
promoter: Sarah / Matthew @ Plum Promotions
info@plummusic.com

BLOOMSBURY THEATRE
15 Gordon Street, London, WC1H 0AH
Tel: 020 7388 8822
blooms.theatre@ucl.ac.uk

THE BOOGALOO
312 Archway Road, Highgate, N6
Tel: 020 8340 2928
Gerry O'Boyle
info@boogaloo.org

THE BORDERLINE
Orange Yard, Manette Street W1D 4JB
(part of Mean Fiddler Group)
Tel: 020 7734 5547
promoter – Barry 020 7534 6956

BOSTON ARMS
178 Junction Road, London N19 5QQ
Tel: 020 7272 8153
Paul Somerville
info@dirtywaterclub.com

BRIXTON ACADEMY
211 Stockwell Road, London SW9 9SL
Tel: 020 7771 3000
Nigel Downs (manager)
nigel@brixton-academy.co.uk
(part of Mckenzie Group)

BRIXTON TELEGRAPH
228 Brixton Hill, Brixton SW2 1HE
Tel: 020 8678 0777
mike@amberlamp.com (promoter)

Buffalo Bar
259 Upper Street, London, N1
Tel: 020 7359 6191
Stacey Thomas
info@buffalobar.co.uk

Bullet Bar
147 Kentish Town Road, NW1 8PB
Adam Marshall
Tel: 020 7485 6040
bar@bulletbar.co.uk

Bull & Gate
389 Kentish Town Road, London, NW5 2TJ
Tel: 020 7093 4820 (external promoter Andy's number, landlord's selling up soon). Their address is: Bull & Gate Promotions, Building A, Trinity Buoy Wharf, 64 Orchard Place, London, E14 0JW

Bush Hall
Bush Hall Music Ltd, 310 Uxbridge Road, London, W12 7LJ
Kath Ratcliffe
Tel: 020 8222 6955
kath@bushhallmusic.co.uk

Caernarvon Castle
7-8 Chalk Farm Road, Camden NW1 8AA,
Tel: 020 72840219
Dan Griffith

Cargo
83 Rivington Street, Shoreditch, EC2A 3AY
Luke.w@cantaloupegroup.co.uk (press officer)
Tel: 020 7613 7732 (Luke Wallace)

Catch
22 Kingsland Road, E2 8DA
Tel: 020 7729 6097
Chandra (promoter, Thursdays only)

Clapham Grand
21-25 st. johns hill, clapham, london, SW11 1TT
marketingandevents@theclaphamgrand.com
Tel: 020 7223 6523

Cobden Club
170-172 Kensal Road, London
W10 5BN
Tel: 020 8960 4222

The Coronet
26-28 New Kent Road, Elephant and Castle, SE16TJ.
Tel: 020 7701 1500.
Manager: John

Dublin Castle
94 Parkway, Camden NW1 7AN
Bugbear Promotions (Jim Mattison and Tony Gleed, external promoters)
info@bugbear18.freeserve.co.uk

Earl's Court
Warwick Road, London, SW5 9TA
Tel: 020 7385 1200

Elbow Rooms
89-91 Chapel Market, Islington N1
Tel: 020 7278 3244
Andy Peyton (promoter)
andypeyton@hotmail.com

Electric Ballroom
184 Camden High Street London NW1
Tel: 020 7485 9007
brian@electricballroom.co.uk (manager)

The End
18 West Central Street, London, WC1A 1JJ
Tel: 020 7419 9199
barbara@endclub.com

The Enterprise
2 Haverstock Hill Chalk Farm London NW3 2BL
Tel: 020 7485 2659

Fabric
77a Charterhouse St, London, EC1M 3HN
Tel: 020 7336 8898
Dan Coshan (general manager)
melissa@fabriclondon.com

Fiddler's Elbow
1 Malden Road, NW5 3HS
Tel: 020 7485 3269 (pub's number)
Alan (promoter of Come Down And Meet The Folks – Sunday afternoons)
goldies@comedownandmeetthefolks.co.uk

Filthy McNasty's Whiskey Bar
68 Amwell Street, Clerkenwell, EC1
Tel: 020 7837 6067
Paul
paul@mediasterling.com

The Forum
9-17 Highgate Road, London NW5
Tel: 020 7284 1001
Ivor Wilkinson or Craig Prentice (managers)
(Mean Fiddler Group)

The Garage
20-22 Highbury Corner, London, N5 1RD
Tel: 020 7607 1818
James Gall (manager)
(Mean Fiddler Group)

Goldsmiths Student Union
Dixon Rd, New Cross, SE14 6NW
Tel: 020 8692 1406
Barry Schooling (entertainment manager)
b.schooling@gold.ac.uk

Gypsy Hill Tavern
79 Gipsy Hill, SE19 1QH
Tel: 020 8761 6533
Owner: Cathy

Halfmoon Putney
Address: 93 Lower Richmond Rd, London SW15
Tel: 020 8780 9383
contact: Carrie Davies
office@halfmoon.co.uk

Hammersmith Apollo
Queen Caroline Street, London, W1
Tel: 020 8563 3800
phil.rogers@clearchannel.co.uk
(manager)

Hammersmith Palais
230 Shepherd Bush Road, London, W6 7NL
Tel: 020 7341 5300
Dave Gaydon
Head of Music & Promotions
Dave.Gaydon@ponana.com

Hope And Anchor
207 Upper St, Islington, N1
Tel: 020 7354 1312
Bugbear Promotions (see Dublin Castle)

ICA
The Mall, SW1 5AH
Tel: 020 7930 3647
Jamie Eastman
andrews@ica.org.uk (Andrew Stewart – administrator)

INFINITY
10 Old Burlington Street W1S 3AG
Tel: 020 7287 5255

ISLINGTON ACADEMY (Carling Academy Islington)
N1 Centre, 16 Parkfield Street London N1 0PS
Tel: 020 7288 4400
Lucinda Brown (Manager)

JAMM (CURRENTLY BAR LORCA)
261 Brixton Road, SW9
Jonathan Allen (owner)
Tel: 020 7274 5537 / 07866 562 377

JAZZ CAFÉ
5 Parkway, Camden Town, London, NW1 7PG
Tel: 020 7916 6060
(Mean Fiddler group)

KOKO
1A Camden High Street, London, NW1 7JE
0870 432 5527
larry@mintgroup.co.uk
(music manager)

Lark In The Park
60 Copenhagen Street, Islington, London N1 0JW
Tel: 020 7278 5781
Sami (landlord)
thelark@tiscali.co.uk

Lock 17
11 East Yard, Camden Lock, NW1 8AB
Matt Wells (manager)
Tel: 020 7428 5929

Madame Jo Jo's
8-10 Brewer's Street, London, W1F 0SP
Tel: 020 7734 3040
Pajoe Saskin (manager)
hireinformation@aol.com

The Marquee
1 Leicester Square, WC2H 7NA
087 0444 6277 (venue number)
(for promoters, see Betsey Trotwood)

Mean Fiddler
157 Charing Cross Road, London WC2H 0EL.
Julie Friel (manager)
management@londonastoria.co.uk

Metro
19-23 Oxford Street, W1R 2DN
Tel: 020 7437 0964
(Promoters Blow-up Metro Paul Tompkin 020 7636 7744)

MONTAGUE ARMS
289 Queens Road, SE15 2PA
Tel: 020 7639 4923
(promoters Fear Of Music Ian 07977 885 712)

NAMBUCCA
596 Holloway Road, N7
Tel: 020 7263 6939
Jay McAllister (promoter)

NEIGHBOURHOOD
12 Acklam Road, W10 5QZ
Tel: 020 7524 7979
info@neighbourhoodclub.net
(promoter Megan 07815 724 879)

NOTTING HILL ARTS CLUB
21 Notting Hill Gate, W11 3JQ
Tel: 020 7598 5226
david@nottinghillartsclub.com
(manager)

ON THE ROCKS
25 Kingsland Road E2 8AA
Tel: 020 7688 0339

PARADISE BAR
460 New Cross Rd, London, SE14 6TJ
John Bundy (new owner, opening again in Feb) 07956 813 587
lovepeacemusic@clara.co.uk (Cathy St Luce)

The Pleasure Unit
359 Bethnal Green Road London E2
Tel: 020 7729 0167
Nick (manager) 07956 291 776
info@pleasureunitbar.com

Purple Turtle
61-65 Crowndale Rd, Camden, London, N1
Tel: 020 7383 4976

Royal Festival Hall
(temporarily closing in July, reopening in 2006)
Belvedere Road, London, SE1 8XX
Tel: 020 7921 0600

Rhythm Factory
16-18 Whitechapel Road, Shoreditch E2
Tel: 020 7375 3774
manager: Alex
rhythmfactory@yahoo.com

Rock Garden
Rock Garden, 6/7 The Piazza, Covent Garden, London WC2E 8HA
Tel: 0207 257 8626
lisa@platformmusic.net (live music promoter)
info@rockgarden.co.uk (venue)

Royal Albert Hall
Kensington Gore, London, SW7 2A
Tel: 020 7589 3203
jessicas@royalalberthall.com (marketing)

The Royal Standard
1 Blackhorse Lane, London E17 6DS
Tel: 020 8503 2523
thestandard@btinternet.com

The Scala
275 Pentonville Road Kings Cross, London, N1 9NL
Tel: 020 7833 2022
ryan@scala-london.co.uk (manager)

Shepherd's Bush Empire
Shepherds Bush, Green London W12
Tel: 020 8354 3300
helen@shepherds-bush-empire.co.uk (manager's assistant)
(part of Mackenzie Group)

Sound
Sound, Swiss Centre Leicester Square, London W1D 6QF
Tel: 020 7287 1010
info@thetalentscout.co.uk
Helen (live music promoter)

Southern K
205 Kilburn High Road, NW6 7HY
info@thedirtyrider.com (promoters)
Tel: 020 8245 0607 (dirty rider club number)

The Spitz
The Spitz. 109 Commercial St. Old Spitalfields Market. London. E1 6BG
Tel: 020 7247 9747
Martin Wissenburg (manager)
martin@spitz.co.uk

ST MORITZ
161 Wardour Street, W1F 8WJ
Tel: 020 7437 0525
sweetie@stmoritz.virgin.net
Gaz Mayall
615a Harrow Road, London, W10 4RA
Tel/Fax: +44 (0)20 8960 4258
E-mail : gaz@gazrockin.com
Web : www.gazrockin.com

TROUBADOUR CLUB
263-7 Old Brompton Road, SW5 9JA
Tel: 020 7370 1434
Simon + Susie Thornhill (owners)
amanda@troubadour.co.uk (music promoter)

ULU
(University Of London Union)
Malet Street, Bloomsbury, WC1E 7HY
Tel: 020 7664 2085
Laurie Pegg (manager)
laurie.pegg@ulu.lon.ac.uk

UNDERWORLD
174 Camden High Street, London NW1
Tel: 020 7482 1932
contact@theunderworldcamden.co.uk

Rock London 2006

THE VENUE
2 Clifton Rise, New Cross, SE14 6JP
Tel: 020 8692 4077
dance@thevenuelondon.com
Richard Evans (acting manager)

WATER RATS
328 Grays Inn Road, London WC1X 8BZ
Tel: 020 7336 7326
(see Betsey Trotwood for music promoters contact)

WEMBLEY ARENA
Stadium Way, Wembley, HA9 0DW
Colin Roberts (marketing)
Tel: 020 8585 3536 (colin roberts' direct line)

WEST ONE FOUR/THE FOX
3 North End Crescent, West Kensington, W14 8TG
Tel: 020 7603 7006

THE WINDMILL
22 Blenheim Gardens, Brixton, SW2 5BZ
Tel: 020 8671 0700
windmillbrixton@yahoo.co.uk
promoter: Tim Perry 020 8674 0055

OTHER INFORMATION

(Head Office Of Mean Fiddler)
Mean Fiddler Music Group plc
16 High Street
Harlesden
London
NW10 4LX
Tel: 020 89615490
tania@meanfiddler.co.uk (group press)

(Head office of McKenzie Group)
McKENZIE GROUP LTD POSTAL ADDRESS
McKenzie Group Ltd
211 Stockwell Road
London SW9 9SL
Tel: 0207 787 3131
louise@mkg.co.uk (press for whole group)

ROCK LONDON
The Definitive Guide
2007

Trevor Baker

Order NOW!

Rock London is being constantly updated
The 2007 edition will be available from Summer 2006.

Order direct from Aureus Publishing on 01656 880033
or online from www.aureus.co.uk or from any online
bookstore. Also available from good bookshops.

ISBN 1-899750-37-1 (ISBN 13: 978-1-899750-37-5)

ONLY £9.99

If you like rock music then you'll love this...

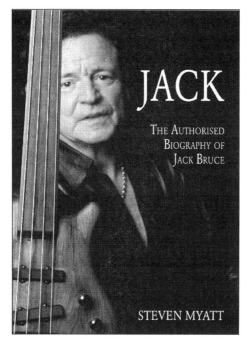

Title: JACK
Subtitle: The Authorised Biography of Jack Bruce
Author : Steven Myatt
ISBN-10 : 1-899750-36-3
ISBN-13 : 978-1-899750-36-8
Publication date: 3rd October 2005
Price: £17.99
No. pages: 256
No. Illustrations : 40 mono photographs
Size: Royal Octavo
Binding : Casebound/Hardback
Classification: Rock and Roll

On November 26 1968, at The Royal Albert Hall, the rock band Cream played their farewell concert. Although only together for a little over two years, they had established themselves as one of Britain's most exciting, innovative and important bands. Cream created a jazz/blues/rock fusion which re-defined contemporary music. All three were hugely talented musicians in their own right, and their music had authority and, above all else, unparalleled power and drive.

Then, in May 2005, they returned. To the huge surprise and delight of their millions of fans, they played four gigs in one week – back at The Royal Albert Hall. For many it was almost beyond belief that a reunion would ever happen. The tickets sold out in record time, and fans came from all over the world.

After the 1968 farewell concert, Cream's bass player, vocalist and co-songwriter, Jack Bruce, quickly created a new and hugely successful solo career – starting with his greatly admired 'Songs For A Tailor' album. Since then he has played with some of the most respected musicians in the world, has released many albums and performed live in front of several million people. Through the late Seventies and Eighties though his life was blighted by drink and drugs problems. During this period his first marriage collapsed and he also had to endure the death of his eldest son. In the autumn of 2003 he survived potentially fatal complications following a liver transplant.

Born in Glasgow in 1943 into a poor and politically very active family, Jack was recognised as a gifted musician from an early age. He studied composition at the Royal Scottish Academy of Music and developed a broad musical taste. When he was still only sixteen, in any one week he would be playing with a jazz band, a country and western group and a full-scale orchestra – and be composing classical music. He bought his first car months before he was old enough to drive it; already earning more than his father. His passions, he says, were music, girls and cars.

In the early Sixties he moved from the acoustic bass to the electric bass and was caught up in the emerging London r 'n b scene. He rapidly gained a formidable reputation as a very powerful and creative player, with a highly distinctive style.

A biography of Jack Bruce is long overdue. Working very closely with Jack – and the huge number of people who have known him and worked with him over the past forty-five years – Steven Myatt has now written that book. It includes a large number of personal photographs which have never been seen before, and will be the first biography of this uniquely talented man – let alone the first authorised biography.

Publisher: Aureus Publishing Limited, Castle Court, Castle-upon-Alun,
St. Bride's Major, Vale of Glamorgan, CF32 0TN. Tel: (01656) 880033
email: sales@aureus.co.uk www.aureus.co.uk

...and this...

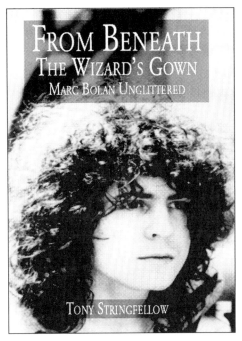

Title: From Beneath the Wizard's Gown
Subtitle: Marc Bolan Unglittered
Author : Tony Stringfellow
ISBN-10 : 1-899750-33-9
ISBN-13 : 978-1-899750-33-7
Publication date: 3 October 2005
Price: £17.99
No. pages: 224
No. Illustrations : 40 mono photographs
Size: Royal Octavo
Binding : Casebound/Hardback
Classification: Rock and Roll

The father of glam rock, Marc Bolan, was renowned for glitter, make-up, camp clothes and performances. His music evolved from ethereal, Tolkenesque influences to stylistically original pop. He died at a time when his persona was still engulfed in the commercialisation of the pop character he had created, leaving the full enigma of his mind untold.

Much has been written about Marc Bolan the 'Glam Rock King' but little has touched on the person below the make-up. This book aims to do just that, inspired by a large selection of previously unpublished poetry of Bolan's, reflecting his earlier works in 'The Warlock of Love'. From Beneath the Wizard's Gown endeavours to delve into the corners of Bolan's mind that made him the charismatic, mystical icon who wrote apparently senseless lyrics. This book aspires to restore a depth of understanding to his words, enhancing his credibility as an artist, a wordsmith and a musician.

The poetry, written in Bolan's own hand, has been aesthetically reproduced from its original form with an edited 'translation' of each poem giving an interpretation of what are perceived to have been Bolan's intended words.

Enigmatic imagery, previously unpublished photographs of Bolan, depicting the naturally ethereal aura he possessed, punctuate the pages of this encompassing, tactile probe into the roots of Bolan's thoughts, that made him the intriguing Wizard-like character who enchanted the music world with his lingual painting of mystical images.

This book aspires to look into the eyes of Marc Bolan, unglittered.

Publisher: Aureus Publishing Limited, Castle Court, Castle-upon-Alun, St. Bride's Major, Vale of Glamorgan, CF32 0TN. Tel: (01656) 880033
email: sales@aureus.co.uk www.aureus.co.u